Galena, Illinois

THE SHINING BROW
FRANK LLOYD WRIGHT

BOOKS BY OLGIVANNA LLOYD WRIGHT

THE SHINING BROW—FRANK LLOYD WRIGHT

OUR HOUSE

THE STRUGGLE WITHIN

Frank Lloyd Wright gave the name Taliesin to a gentle Wisconsin hill rising above the running stream and green meadows. Later he identified that name with the home he built as an adorning brow around the hill's crown.

Taliesin—The Shining Brow—was the name of a Welsh bard who sang songs to beauty. Mr. Wright liked the poet; he liked the melodious sound of the name, and he liked its meaning—The Shining Brow—the symbol of dignity, purity, nobility, all of the finest human attributes.

To me Frank Lloyd Wright is synonymous with Taliesin. It is he who is The Shining Brow—the epitome of creative force in a life devoted to beauty.

THE SHINING BROW
FRANK LLOYD WRIGHT

OLGIVANNA LLOYD WRIGHT

HORIZON PRESS   NEW YORK   1960

(The kind help of those who have made their photographs available is here gratefully acknowledged: John Amarantides, Allan Davison, John Engstead, P. E. Guerrero and John Howe.)

Dedicated to the Taliesin Fellowship

CONTENTS

Prologue   *page* 15

PART ONE   OUR LIFE

1   New York   21
2   Taliesin West—Arizona   43
3   Taliesin North—Wisconsin   61
4   Taliesin West—Arizona   91
5   Taliesin North—Wisconsin   124

PART TWO   OUR WORK

6   Frank Lloyd Wright's Letter to the
    University of Wichita   149
7   Fellowship   153
8   The Garden   168
9   The Guggenheim Museum   171
10 The Beth Sholom Synagogue   189

PART THREE   REMINISCENCES

11   197

PART FOUR   REFLECTIONS

12   253
13   257
14   262
15   267
16   279
17   282
18   286
19   289
20   292
        Epilogue   295

ILLUSTRATIONS

Mr. and Mrs. Frank Lloyd Wright   *frontispiece*
Mrs. Wright with Iovanna   *page* 37
Svetlana   37
Mr. Wright with Iovanna   37
Two family picnic scenes   38
Taliesin, Wisconsin   71
Taliesin West, Arizona   71
Mrs. Wright and Trixie   72
Mr. Wright and Johnny Walker   72
Riding in the Lectracar-Surrey   72
Taliesin Fellowship weeding the Flower Triangle   105
A performance of *Patience*   105
Festival of Music and Dance   105
Tea with the Fellowship in the desert   106
Eugene Masselink and William Wesley Peters
   with Mr. Wright   106
Monthly presentation of drawings   139
The Fellowship at work in the drafting room   139
Mr. and Mrs. Wright   140

PROLOGUE

June 8, 1869 will forever mark the beginning of a new epoch for the world. It marks the day of a great poet who quenched the thirst of those that wished to achieve the highest form of beauty it is possible to realize during the sojourn on earth. The world received his benediction in art and architecture and in a deep philosophy of life which has for its base the integrity of the individual.

On June 8, 1869 a great gift was bestowed upon America and the world. The gift of a man who forcefully made his way through his contemporaries and then led them to the creative forms of a way of life which liberated man from being imprisoned in his own dwelling. He took them to the freedom of space and called to them—that all is one. He declared that the spirit and the body are one because the spirit consumes the body for its service. And he declared that man and his house are one. The exterior form of the building is born from within outward. It is the space within which determines the reality of the building. It is the world within that is the real world of man.

June 8th marks the birth of Frank Lloyd Wright—

who dedicated his life to an ideal held high out of reach of those who unwittingly might have damaged it.

"I don't think that all is matter or all is mind," he said. "The great thing, the great thought in it all—the thing to hang on to is—all is one.

"There is no division, there is no elemental antagonism between what we call body and mind. We have been accustomed to separating time and space, and all other such concepts. They are primitive and we have had to use them in order to get hold of anything at all intellectually. An intellectual concept is always limited, as the box is, compared with the organic sense of disseminating building into space. Do you see space as something definite appearing to you? Is it an emptiness? Is it something to be inhabited? What is it? Can you envision it?

"Soul is the same. No one can picture to himself his soul. Now the question is whether this aspect of form which we wear, which we call our bodies, is any more real or half as real, or in any sense approximately so real as this thing that we cannot imagine, cannot see, and yet—is. How do you know that matter is different from the spirit, and that the spirit is not as real as this stone under your feet—or the air you breathe?

"The world of the body is the real world of most people because they have not yet learned better. They would never agree with you that your spirit and your body are one. All you need to worry about is that— all is one. You cannot take it apart. The moment you attempt to take it apart, just then is when you would begin to fail. You could not become masters of Organic

16

Architecture. You could not proceed from within outward. If you work to create something, you must have essential understanding which proceeds from an inner sense of beauty, of life, of reality."

He sang his hymns to the beauty of creation because he saw Nature as divine representation, as divine reflection of the Great Creator.

In every blade of grass, in every grain of sand, he saw the exalting beauty of divine spirit. He moved on earth with power of faith which destroyed every obstacle in his way. The material world held inner meaning for him, transforming it into poetry every second of his breath on earth.

The tears of sorrow and suffering lay gently over his spirit as the dew lies on the grass glistening with sunlight in the early hours of the morning.

The tears of his suffering and sorrow were illumined by love. The forgiveness of his heart was so formidable that he held not a glimmer of resentment against his enemies. They always remained outside of his inner world. He obtained this without effort, he simply felt no evil as evil.

But he would let nothing touch his ideal. He fought those who attempted to tear it down. But he fought them without evil in his heart. And he fought for truth without evil in his heart.

His spirit grew to a limitless stature. He consumed the ninety years of his life in the service of mankind and therefore in the service of himself. He stood among us to show us perhaps what a man could really be like if he would but serve an ideal higher than himself. His

17

Creator called him back. And now we may, through missing his presence on earth, finally learn a great truth about ourselves. By missing him we may at last use our resources within to lead us to union with his spirit, and maybe at last we will understand that life is the echo of death.

PART ONE

OUR LIFE

Chapter I

NEW YORK

On November 10th, 1958, before leaving Wisconsin for our Arizona winter headquarters, Mr. Wright and I had dinner with the Taliesin Fellowship in our living room. William T. Evjue of the Madison, Wisconsin, *Capital Times* came to spend that evening with us all. It was our last evening in Wisconsin with Mr. Wright in our midst.

For some reason, although there were ninety people in the living room, our dinner was unusually quiet. The ensemble played, the choir sang, Gunnar Johannsen, the well-known pianist, played Bach's Piano Concerto and Fugue. The long Bechstein piano became a full orchestra, reverberating throughout Taliesin.

When Mr. Johannsen stopped playing, the atmosphere of the room shook with spontaneous applause. A long time afterward, small groups of people sat talking in a lively manner, still carrying on, sharing the impressions of the evening. Mr. Wright and I went quietly to our rooms. We read for a while, still hearing the distant pleasing hum of voices in our living room.

In the morning a big Northwest Airlines plane carried us to New York. That same evening Mr. Wright and I went to the International Festival of Art in the Seagram Building, which is set some 100 feet back from Park Avenue on a plaza raised up about five feet, like old monumental buildings. It was built by Internationalist Mies van der Rohe. Approaching it was a peculiar experience: One felt that it had all the ingredients to make it a great building, but somehow, somewhere, it missed.

Mr. Wright remarked, "Although this building should be dated nineteenth century, it is the best the internationalists have produced. Mies van der Rohe has come closest to the ideal of negation as a cliché."

The structure is of dark brown, almost black, bronze, which gives it a funereal aspect. It seems to be the symbol of pessimism, a tomb—a monument to the dying city.

The water in the pools at the base is raised two feet above the platform on which the building stands—a reactionary protest against the natural—utter artificiality being apotheosis. "I have seen many materials misused before," Mr. Wright said, "but never until now have I seen water misused."

The interior is enclosed in glass. The elevator enclosures are boxed in cream-colored travertine, an Italian marble which here ineffectually resembles plain plastered walls at about ten times the cost of genuine plaster!

Tom Lee, designer of the Festival Galleries, and David Eliott, the coordinator of the Festival, escorted us through the Exhibition.

Unfortunately, the modern paintings of such countries even as Indonesia, Bolivia, Argentina, Finland and

22

the Union of South Africa, are affected by the French decadent trend in painting. They produced an effect of Madame Tussaud's Wax Works as we moved from one room to another. Glaring out of the frames were nudes holding hands with skeletons, deformed bodies, disfigured faces—a pile of cubes and squares with displaced arms, and eyes peeking from under the pile. Even the cubes were distorted.

Within crooked walls of a room an artist had painted massive bodies sitting squalidly in chairs—supposedly human males and females. Our eyes fell on blank, vacant faces. Sensuality was offered as grace in bodies of sharp, shocking colors. Paste-like faces, pale green, depraved, with grotesque ugly eyes staring in dumb, baboon expressions. Even the children in the pictures looked miserable, with flesh hanging like a deflated balloon on their frames. Not a happy modern picture in the whole exhibition! The hopeless, depraved, mournful side of human existence was accentuated. Disintegration—both of the soul and the body.

But in one partition all by itself stood proudly a candelabrum called "The Menorah" made of metal by Ludwig Wolpert, an Israeli artist. Mr. Wright and I sat in front of it to relieve our eyes in the grace and faultless beauty of this religious symbol. The candelabrum stood five feet tall and four and a half feet wide, with three branches of wrought iron on each side and the seventh in the center. White candles were ready to be lighted. The only modern declaration of faith from a foreign country.

The other beautiful works of art came from China, Japan, Iran and Holland, dating back hundreds of years. A marvelous head of Buddha, superb Japanese screens, belonging to all time. A magnificent Rembrandt with his unmatched technique and life.

And then we entered the room where Mr. Wright's models, photographs and drawings were displayed; these, like the Israeli symbol, vibrated with faith, love and force uncorrupted; genuinely American through and through. He had been chosen as the only artist to represent the United States of America. The model of the Price Tower stood strong against a tall glass window, putting the silhouette of faceless skyscrapers in the street to shame. The Tower seemed to be a waterfall arrested in motion. There were the spread wings of the Johnson house; the Lloyd Lewis house, self-contained, reposing amidst the trees; the Monona Terrace, harmonious, quiet, waiting to be brought into life.

By the time we reached this room the crowd around Mr. Wright was so thick that I could hardly see him.

Later as we walked silently along Park Avenue I thought of what our world had become—a world of high pressure advertisement, of salesmanship, of the continuous hypnotic effect of what others have to say about us and everything we do. We are beginning to lose our own individual reactions. Our spontaneity is being numbed in a maze of words constantly buffeting us. To judge what is beautiful, truly from our own inner sense of beauty, is becoming increasingly difficult.

Walking beside Mr. Wright, I thought, he is right— our safety does lie in the study of Nature, in that deep sense of integral unity. Artificiality of life is rushing upon us in such rapid strides that to preserve our natural reactions has become a disciplinary work which needs our constant attention.

To watch the growth of rockets and bombs, to realize that, with all the gifts offered us on earth, we spend most of our effort and ingenuity in promoting destruction, cripples the spirit. To read of the talks of war and peace, and whether force should be met by force, while nations scheme to grab one another's land, to threaten war . . .

What good can come of it? Can we not yet realize that it is no longer a matter of speculation? We have long passed that point. The phrase "war or peace" should be substituted by "death or survival"; there can be no survival for anyone in our highly imaginative modes of destruction. Peace now is a command for all mankind. But what is disheartening is that this command did not originate in faith, love and an ideal, but in man's new, mad, fanatical devotion to science, in his pursuit of the quickest and highest death-rate obtainable—the suicide of the human race. Fear is a grotesque force that drives us into confusion of all values, consuming the reason and the power of judgment—segregating the divine potentialities within our soul from us.

The following day Mr. Wright had a luncheon engagement with William Zeckendorf, the urban reconstruction operator. When he returned he described the whole occasion to me. He had gone up to Mr. Zeckendorf's splendid twelfth floor apartment-offices on Madison Avenue, which were completely equipped with facilities to dine and entertain clients in the corner of the roof garden.

The subject which naturally arose was: saving the city. Mr. Wright maintained that cities have reached the point where they are not worth saving. "What we need most are intelligent efforts to decentralize the big city and start new ones."

The conversation went on to the rehabilitation of property in the heart of New York. Mr. Wright said that such buildings as are now going up in New York will only increase the traffic and create a greater problem than already exists—adding traffic jam to traffic jam; they are not saving the city, but giving it a final kick into oblivion.

Being a large-scale operator all over the country, Mr. Zeckendorf had secured a portion of the Santa Monica Hills near Los Angeles. He and his staff were studying the problem of developing the housing in such a way as to afford Los Angeles a little breathing area. This idea seemed to be good but the plan was to pile the inhabitants into concentrated heaps, higher and higher, narrower and narrower, in order to leave some green space to look down upon from the concentrations; in other words, planting skyscrapers all over the hills.

"In 1927 I conceived the skyscraper to be built in the country—the proper place for it," Mr. Wright spoke. "Later I built the Price Tower in the prosperous village of Bartlesville, Oklahoma. But the exaggeration of that idea is *reductio ad absurdum*. Instead of putting an end to pig-piling, it seems to be growing into a confirmed habit throughout the nation. In the Price Tower—so far so good. But multiplying it as a unit in a universal building system—as a proposition that is preposterous!

26

For instance, the teenager problem looming in this country cannot be solved that way.

"It seems that the agronomy natural to our Democracy is being reduced to mendicant by this urban craze. The natural tendency of humanity toward the gregarious is being unfairly stimulated and exaggerated for profit. America desperately needs planning in the opposite direction. We still seem to be suffering from the aftermath of the Civil War when the 'cinderstrip' wiped out culture on the green. Instead of the great green pastures, we now have placed the center of gravity on the long green banknotes. Where is salvation coming from?

"Even hotels are being leveled to the mediocrity of ordinary business. With the building of luxury motels, connected with beautiful spacious greenery and scenery, hotels as they now are will become a thing of the past, I hope and believe. The proper luxury motels in the country will also help gradually to remove from the city the congestion which is now choking it."

Mr. Wright liked big generous William Zeckendorf with his earthy sense of humor. He and all of us at Taliesin were moved when Mr. Zeckendorf saved the Robie House in Chicago, an early landmark of Mr. Wright's work, which in 1957 was in danger of being torn down.

Our week in New York was filled with engagements. When we went to dinner at Alicia and Harry Guggenheim's we met again some of our old friends. Ruddy Carl Sandburg; the now gray-haired Robert Hutchins and his dainty wife—Dr. Hutchins is the former presi-

dent of the University of Chicago and now heads The
Fund for the Republic—and Al Shaw, a Chicago architect who had designed a $27,000,000 federal building
on the lake front; there was also a newspaperwoman
from *Newsday*. Dr. Hutchins asked Carl Sandburg:
"Which do you think has greater influence on the
American people, the government or the newspapers?"

"Under Roosevelt the government had more influence; under Eisenhower the newspapers have," answered Mr. Sandburg. All appeared to agree with him.

They then teased our hostess, Alicia Patterson Guggenheim, the publisher of *Newsday*, about her influence
upon the people of America.

"Men resist the influence of women in any field," I
remarked. "In ancient Egypt woman was above man,
she then became equal, then inferior, and now the cycle
is rising again; she is equal and at present, if I may say
so, there is also a striving for superiority on her part.
That is why the tension between men and women is
tightening today—men resist this imminent danger to
their position as leaders."

"I believe you are right," our hostess said thoughtfully. At the other end of the table, someone was saying,
"If a wife has no influence upon her husband there must
be something wrong with him."

Since most of those present were newspaper people,
they dropped into nostalgic reminiscences of their experiences. "I was offered the job of managing editor of
the *Chicago American*," related Dr. Hutchins, "so I
went to see William Randolph Hearst. I told him there
was not one good newspaper in the whole city of Chicago. Mr. Hearst interrupted me in his high falsetto:

'Maybe Chicago gets what it deserves. Sometimes people don't understand the newspaper business. I was travelling on a train once when I met Charles Eliot, the president of Harvard University and I asked him what newspaper he admired most. He answered in cold blood that he thought most highly of the *London Times.*' Mr. Hearst paused a moment, then spoke triumphantly with a dark smile: 'The *London Times* sold out a few weeks later!' "

"My, my," said Carl Sandburg, with exaggerated appreciation, "so you actually saw William Randolph Hearst in the flesh?"

"Would you like to shake the hand that shook the hand of William Randolph Hearst?" said Dr. Hutchins, striking a dramatic attitude.

"Think what Chicago would have been like if you had been the editor of the *Chicago American* while Lloyd Lewis was the editor of the *Daily News?* The word 'racketeer' would not be known in our vocabulary," spoofed Carl Sandburg.

"Did you ever hear the story about Lloyd Lewis and a certain distinguished visitor from London?" asked Dr. Hutchins. "The three of us, with Carl here, were sitting in the University Restaurant when Lloyd's wife, Kathryn, joined us. Carl was describing for the visitor from London the terrible condition of crime in Chicago. Gang violence was rampant on every street corner! Lloyd became quite heated in defense of his city. He assured the visitor that reports of crime in Chicago were greatly exaggerated. 'It's a shame,' Lloyd said, 'that Chicago has such a vile reputation. In reality it is one of the safest cities in America!' The visitor appreciated this new angle and believed that Lloyd, since he was a prominent newspaperman, must know what he was talking about. Shortly after that, Lloyd and Kathryn bade us goodbye, and I stayed on with our guest. It could not have been more than twenty minutes later when they both reappeared in the doorway, distracted. 'My God! Kathryn and I have just been held up—robbed!' Lloyd grunted. 'They took Kathryn's mink coat and her diamond bracelet! Quick! Call the police!' It did not occur to us to laugh. We called the police but the mink coat and the diamond bracelet were never recovered—the crime was perfect!"

"Lloyd was a wonderful, rare man," our beautiful hostess remembered with sadness. Mr. Wright said, "He was a brother to me." We all felt that he was our friend and I, especially, was happy to have had the privilege of claiming him as a friend. He left our world much too soon. We need spirits like his.

"Yes, Lloyd *was* rare," Mr. Wright said. "He was a real American. He always reminded me, 'Don't be too hard on them, Frank; never forget, Life takes all kinds.'"

Our hostess presided at the table with her natural, easy charm. When she had invited us to dinner, she had asked what Mr. Wright would like to have; and she served a delicious crown roast because it was his favorite dish.

After dinner we moved into the drawing room where Carl Sandburg played his guitar and sang for us. American ballads filled the air. Carl Sandburg's deep voice changed the room into the wind-rippled fields of

corn and wheat that stretch far into the vast, endless
American prairies.

In addition to all the work, conferences and engagements, Mr. Wright and I both worked on our manuscripts for forthcoming books with our publisher, Ben
Raeburn of the Horizon Press. He would frequently
work with me first and after a long session, when I was
barely able to stand on my feet, he would then begin
to work with Mr. Wright until late hours of the evening. I would usually have to step in and take command of the situation, virtually ordering them to stop
and go get a bite to eat. After dinner, Ben Raeburn had
to drive to his home in Long Island.

Although gentle of nature, Mr. Raeburn is firm and
persistent, works hard and drives his authors to the
last drop of their energy. He is mercilessly demanding
in a very agreeable manner.

His admiration for Mr. Wright, for his architecture
and for his writings has no bounds. Mr. Wright considered him among his most faithful friends. Ben Raeburn
has been the sole publisher of all of Mr. Wright's works
since 1953. I have learned from him what work is involved in publishing one single book. The publisher
works with the author in editing and reading. Together
they select the quality of paper, binding, and the type
face itself. This is followed by meticulous proofreading
and revising until at last the book is ready to go to
press. Simultaneously he arranges for the design of the
jacket cover. Meanwhile the vast machinery of distribu-
tion and advertisement begins to get under way.

The publisher inevitably has his headaches, arguments, worries, clashes and disappointments with some of his more stubborn authors. I myself fought, but justifiably of course, for some pet word, phrase, or just for a plain comma! He patiently pressed his point and usually I had to give in—at least I always thought so.

He and his beautiful wife Pearl have become the friends of Taliesin. Mr. Wright was very fond of gentle, sensitive, and devoted Ben Raeburn.

During this busy visit in New York, Bud Lewis, a competent young writer for the Dave Garroway television program came to interview Mr. Wright in preparation for NBC's eighth anniversary. He was quiet and reticent of manner. Interviewing for a broadcast in a general way is the usual ritual, although Mr. Wright always told them it was not necessary for him. But, of course, no one could believe this to be true. Mr. Lewis asked Mr. Wright challenging questions: what he thought of the atom bomb, of New York City, of the International style, of skyscrapers, etc.

"The atom bomb is only a symptom of the condition of our civilization," Mr. Wright declared. "The bomb is the consequence of the scientific spree. Owing to that, our future is hanging by a thread—it may disappear but the good of humanity will never perish.

"As to New York City? It shows what a London dormitory town might have done if only it had the money! New York will inevitably dwindle to its end. It is the office of the architect to see life as more natural, more free, and to lead his people to a more humane use of its scientific advantages. We ought to start again. Art, architecture and religion are obscured by science.

Science has already pushed us to the brink. Even the Church has dwindled to a form of sectarianism. The spirit of man has been less and less the beneficiary of the new idea America proclaimed—the sovereignty of the individual. We once had prophets like Walt Whitman, Thoreau, Thomas Jefferson . . . hardly anyone reads them now and very few understand their significance as prophetic. Today we pay homage to profit—this is our religion; money is increasingly our power and it now belongs to the third generation authoritarian who disseminates this power without the knowledge of principle, not having been educated properly in the ethics of Democracy. We have too long ignored the integrity of beauty, sacrificing the prophetic to profit.

"Internationalism, a graft of my own work gone wrong, is the same violation of nature. It strips architecture of beauty, choking it by mass-production with no character, no sense, the ultimate aim being profit.

"As to skyscrapers? The skyscraper is more appropriate in the country because it has plenty of space, crowds no one, and casts a shadow on its own ground. The skyscraper in the city is an urban blight on human existence. I got sick of those dead boxes, that is why I designed a genuinely economic and structurally sound skyscraper a mile high—a city in itself of about 130,000 people."

At eight o'clock the following morning Mr. Lewis picked us up at the Plaza apartment and escorted us to the NBC building where we all huddled in an informal way waiting for Mr. Wright's turn. We ran into

Thomas Hart Benton, the American painter, who exchanged words with Mr. Wright before his own appearance on the same program. Mr. Wright chided him about his pipe, "How long have you been following your pipe around, Tom?"

"Fifty years," answered Tom Hart, unbaffled.

"Well, I bet if you wrapped wet sheets around yourself in a Turkish bath they would come off bright yellow."

"It stops me from talking too much, though," laughed Thomas Benton. "I have a genius for talking, you know."

"If you apply the word genius to talkers, I guess the country is full of them," Mr. Wright said.

He continued: "How do you like the New York style carpenter-architecture in steel? It is back in the nineteenth century, don't you think? They had no steel then, but the architects of today cannot get out of their old wood habits, and they still build steel as wood— the old post and beam construction. The carpenter did not know how to negotiate corners except with the square, thus square buildings and vertical walls. Yet there is no square in nature—nature knows only rounded forms. The museum directors have been hanging paintings on vertical walls in square rooms, and calling that the 'rectilinear frame of reference.' They cannot get over it yet. Do you like to hang your paintings in the 'rectilinear frame of reference,' Tom?"

"I don't care what I hang them on," shouted Tom Benton. "The architects give us square walls, so we hang our paintings square. You can bust that idea if you want to."

"I guess we will have to bust the museum directors first," Mr. Wright remarked, and they both hilariously enjoyed themselves.

Mr. Wright went to be televised, and Bud Lewis graciously took me to a small room to watch the television screen. Mr. Wright looked noble and handsome, and his talk was like fresh mountain streams.

"I believe he is the greatest man living today," Bud Lewis whispered to me with quiet conviction.

One day of the same week we decided to visit the Beth Sholom Synagogue which Mr. Wright designed for Elkins Park, a suburb of Philadelphia. Driving to Pennsylvania Station, Mr. Wright pointed out to me the massive columns standing free in space above the taxi entrance, supporting nothing. "Look," he said. "All this is a conspicuous waste."

"Why did the architect put them there?" I asked.

"For decoration, I guess, but nobody ever looks up there. They are superfluous from every point of view—a great vacancy and uselessness just for imposing effect."

Our son-in-law, Wesley Peters, who accompanied us said, "Similar columns were bad enough in the Baths of Caracalla in Rome but these modern copies are simply ridiculous for a twentieth-century railroad station."

We entered the gigantic station which only a few years ago was divided into sections to utilize some of its waste space and to protect the personnel and passengers from severe drafts. But it was still very drafty and we nearly froze waiting for the train in the immense gloom.

We walked into the dining car as the first passengers amid the silent grim waiters and their steward. "No one recognized you," I said to Mr. Wright with gladness, and we suddenly felt at ease and relaxed. We saw some bridges in the distance and Mr. Wright was reminded of an incident in Japan. "An American asked a Japanese engineer why the Ryogoku bridge collapsed. The Japanese bowed slightly and answered with a polite smile, 'Honorable decimal point—he in wrong place.'"

Our builder, Haskell Culwell, met us at the North Philadelphia Station and drove us up Broad Street, which Philadelphians claim to be the longest main street in the world. A soft-spoken Oklahoman, Mr. Culwell had built several buildings designed by Mr. Wright: the Price Tower in Bartlesville, houses in Phoenix and Oklahoma, and now the Synagogue.

"There it is!" He pointed to the building as it rose in the distance like a frozen mountain. Approaching it slowly we could watch this unbelievable edifice shimmering like showers of melted diamonds. It was reminiscent of Mount Sinai, exalted in glory of faith in Man and God. It stood above the rush of the city streets around it. Alone, proud as a mountain is proud, self declared, sanctified by beauty, it remained apart from the world. Yet one felt attracted toward it as by some great force calling silently to partake of its quiet splendor. The sheets of concrete, the glass and cast aluminum, were brilliantly crisp in the early afternoon sun.

Mr. Wright
with Iovanna.

Svetlana.

Mrs. Wright
and Iovanna.

Mr. and Mrs. Wrigh
with Svetlana (le
and Iovanna (cente
on a family picnic
the valley below Ta
esin, Wisconsin.

An outing, with M
and Mrs. Wright,
vanna and (in bac
ground, left) John
Koven Hill.

As we entered the vestibule of the building, the perforated intersecting planes above our heads were extensions of the planes from the central part of the Synagogue and composed the roof of the interior entrance. These openings flowed from one part of the building to another giving the whole edifice unity of motion.

There was no separation felt as we climbed the gradual low concrete steps into the central hall of the Synagogue. On its two far sides, thrust high into the sky, were prow-like, triangular wings which accented the space with their fine lines. Three wide uprising clear spans supported the main pyramidal tripod of steel and glass. From the ceiling downward extended silver concrete bands with recessed triangular patterns and sheets of cream white plastic. The light that sweeps from all sides through frosted glass from the great ceiling down, gives an illusion of up and down motion. A soft silver light permeates the whole interior with a meditative quality that asks for peaceful silence.

A huge triangular form of glass and metal, suspended from the center of the ceiling on long chains, looked as though it were descending from the sky itself. The triangle was studded with slender electric lights interspersed on different planes. The rest of the ceiling was covered with delicate stalactite-shaped lights.

Six concrete steps led up to the dais in the back center of which was the Ark with carved walnut doors containing the Torahs. Close to the front on each side of the dais stood the Menorahs, the seven-branched candelabra, of cast aluminum, designed by Mr. Wright as all was designed by him. Above the Ark were symbolic silver wings spreading horizontally to the ornamental concrete and metal screens, studded with clusters of tiny lights and backed by red velvet and gold curtains. The music of the organ came through these screens. From the center of the dais hung the sacred traditional Everlasting Light over the carved walnut lecterns and the table for the Torah.

We then went to the secluded and beautifully proportioned Wedding Chapel below, which was painted a soft cream color and was lighted with triangular fixtures. It seats three hundred people. The Ark containing the Torah was different from the Ark in the main part of the Synagogue. It also was of carved walnut, but the sliding doors had glass inserts which lighted the back of the Ark with a mysterious luminous light. We saw luxurious reception rooms and the bride's chamber which led directly into the Chapel.

A complete, perfectly finished structure is this Synagogue—the new temple of Judaism expressing in organic terms the holy significance of this religious faith. "For the first time Judaism has found a form of its own in America," Mr. Wright remarked.

It was Rabbi Mortimer Cohen's vision and will that made this edifice possible. It took years of his effort, devotion, persistence, and unwavering faith in Mr. Wright, to collect enough money and backing to build this new Synagogue. Through trials of a life dedicated to a cause—a temple of Judaism in its noblest form— he won his hardest battle. The genius of Frank Lloyd Wright has given to him, and to all who stand in faith, the greatest Synagogue in the world.

The crowded week of our stay in New York ended and we were at last on our way to Arizona.

Arthur Pieper, a former member of the Taliesin Fellowship, drove out with us to Idlewild Airport. New York does not look happy at an early hour of the morning; it seemed especially unhappy to us as we drove through the snarl of steel bridges, viaducts and freeways.

Surveying the silhouettes of the criss-cross frames of the buildings, the trucks and cars speeding by, Mr. Wright remarked, "New York is the expression of an era non-comprehensive of the nature of steel as it is non-comprehensive of the nature of the automobile. All these steel bridges, like the skyscrapers you see, are a wasteful way of utilizing an unsuitable site. To do all this—to connect around about—is the confession of a misuse of a site for a city. This whole fabric is just to make up for an initial mistake. Every city is after-the-fact an overgrown village. No city is deliberately planned.

"Washington certainly is that city representing the day when centralization was the only thing they seemed to know. So a cartwheel with its hub seemed the ideal form for a capital.

"These viaducts we are going under, these bridges, like the car, are ludicrous 'expert' exaggerations. The Brooklyn and the George Washington bridges are fine examples of steel being used naturally. But most of the bridges are lumber-designed steel. The engineers only knew how to put lumber together until Roebling came along and showed them how to use steel in tension structurally. He was an intelligent and courageous man.

41

"The city grew haphazardly, developing messily the suburban areas which have now become worse than the downtown. Although a huddle is always hottest at the center, it is even more distressing at the circumference. It is wrong in principle to build those edges as towns to sleep in—and the city to work in.

"Urban extremities in America are murdering the succeeding generations, producing a natural incubator of crime for the teen-ager. It is the city that produced the suburb, and the suburb produces the restless to-and-fro."

"People commute an hour or an hour and a half back and forth from the country or suburbs," said Arthur. "They like it because they catch up on their reading during that time."

"Maybe today it is the only place and time where culture can get a foothold," Mr. Wright said. "The suburban train or the motor car represents social intercourse now."

"How about the Roman cities?" I asked. "Was that centralization better than the cities of today?"

"Yes," Mr. Wright answered. "In Roman times the city was a normal instrument, indispensable means of communication from the outside, at once a meeting place and a cultural center. Now it is merely a hangover habit—mankind's mediocrity and lack of imagination. The lower instincts of humanity began to take their course. The gregarious animal nature never builds up —only levels down. The herd has never been the proper place for culture."

Chapter 2

TALIESIN WEST—ARIZONA

We stopped at the Chicago airport where our daughter, Iovanna, joined us and we continued our flight west. The weather was choppy and our airship quivered, leaped up and slid down the clouds. We were one and a half hours late, and heading toward Phoenix we were virtually blown in by the wind onto the runway.

And after nine and a half hours of flight we were coming down the steps, hanging on for dear life to the rail because the north wind was blowing mercilessly, whipping our coats and tearing the hats off our heads. My brother Vlado and the young people met us with the classic apology, "The weather has been fine here until today. This is the worst wind which has hit us this season. It just started a few minutes before you arrived."

We drove through the familiar streets of Phoenix and Scottsdale, turning off on our Shea Boulevard, two-thirds of which is now blacktop. Only the last third and the Taliesin road, two miles long, which we built ourselves, are still the floor of the desert with some gravel rolled into it.

Our desert home looked lovely, brilliantly lit for our

homecoming, and the young faces all around us were happy to see us once more safely descended from the sky. However, the desert was unfriendly. Grim and clouded, it shed heavy rain which was followed by huge snowflakes that melted instantly as they lighted on the ground. But high on our McDowell Mountain range the snow kept falling without melting, covering the long shoulders of the mountains with a thin blue-white cape extending halfway down the slope.

When we started building the camp in the Arizona desert, Mr. Wright used only stone, redwood and canvas, because the climate was mellow and sunny with very little dampness or rain. But the climate began to grow more severe in the ensuing years and I believed that we should replace the canvas with glass. He did not like to relinquish the idea of a building made of stone, wood and textiles. "But the weather has changed —there are too many cold days, and even the rainy days have increased. This prevents us from opening the canvas flaps and has been forcing us into the use of too much artificial light," I pleaded. "You are the only one in the whole world who will know how to combine glass and canvas. Please put the glass in so we can always see the beauty of the mountains."

But he still wanted to believe that the Arizona climate would change back to what it was thirty years before.

Seven years went by, and one morning I woke up under the fresh impression of a dream. "I dreamed," I told him, "that you had built a long room extending from the Sun Terrace to the Point. The two walls were

44

of solid stone, the other two were huge sheets of glass interrupted by stone piers in long intervals. There was a glittering storm in the desert—the lightning streaked over Camelback Mountain, the wind whirled the clouds, McDowell Range was blue. Diagonal lines of rain slashed its sides. You and I were standing together watching and enjoying the storm."

He smiled very gently, "All right, Mother, we will use glass with the canvas."

"But it is the truth," I exclaimed. "I did have this dream last night." But by then he and the boys were already taking measurements for the glass. And of course he was the only one who could have combined these two materials with such perfect harmony. There was little need to change the lines of the structure. The camp turned into a transparent phantom desert ship with ever moving colors of the plains and mountains.

The remaining canvas flaps have to be replaced every three years; those less exposed to the sun every five or six years. That is easily done, because the frames are removable; our apprentices simply stretch new canvas on frames.

Cornelia Brierly is my right-hand assistant in interior decorating, as she was during Mr. Wright's life with us. In the winter of 1959 we re-upholstered our furniture in the main living room. We bought cotton rugs of red, chartreuse, aquamarine, purple, and did the up-holstering ourselves. Our friends marvel at this ac-complishment. "It is a job of an experienced profes-sional," they say in wonder.

Having worked with Mr. Wright for thirty-four years, I have naturally developed my visual awareness. He often had me choose the color schemes and let me make the furniture arrangements. So it comes quite naturally to me to continue the same work.

We have changed the furniture at Taliesin East and Taliesin West so many times that no one here can remember how it was from year to year. And whenever Mr. Wright and I traveled and stopped at a hotel the first thing we did was to change the furniture around in our rooms. Even if we stayed just two or three days we changed everything. Then we would go and buy flowers, branches or fruit to make the short stay as beautiful as it could be made in an impersonal hotel room.

I claim to have moved, pushed, pulled more furniture than any woman ever did.

But we did not fare too well in Chicago as the guests of our old and close friends, the late Dr. and Mrs. Ferdinand Schevill. When they went out one day and were not to return until evening, Mr. Wright suggested that we change the furniture in their living room. "They have no time to do it themselves. I want to help them," he said.

"Be careful," I warned. "Are you sure they will be pleased?"

"Of course they will," he answered. "We are like a family. We will make their living room beautiful."

So we attacked the work. I even helped him to pull the piano to another place! We moved every piece of furniture and worked until both of us were exhausted. We then went to the flower shop and Mr. Wright carried back a heavy pot of white lilacs while I held an enormous armful of decorative foliage. When he placed the lilacs by the piano and I put the branches on the tables and the mantel, we sat down admiring the fruit of our afternoon's work. The old room now contained the magic of harmony.

When Ferdinand and Clara entered their house, Mr. Wright greeted them happily. "Olgivanna and I fixed your living room for you," he said.

Clara Schevill, a tall, beautiful woman, looked shocked, unbelieving—first at the room, then at Mr. Wright, then at me. I knew that we had lost. Dr. Schevill was kind and tried to say how nice it was. After a few more minutes of uneasy conversation we went to change our clothes. During dinner we talked of everything except the living room.

When in the morning Mr. Wright and I came down to breakfast, the living room was back as we had found it—old, with dispersed, unrelated furniture. During the night Clara and Ferdinand Schevill had moved everything back. They even took the lilac and branches into the hallway. Neither they nor we said a word about it.

And after we left, Mr. Wright said softly, "They could at least have waited until we had gone. I guess Ferdinand and Clara are too set in their habit of living."

"And they are such wonderful people, too," I said. "What a pity they could not rise to your gift. The room was so beautiful."

I shall never forget the miracle of transformation from ugliness to beauty.

47

Upon returning to either Wisconsin or Arizona, we have usually had an influx of new apprentices, so at Taliesin West we now had to extend the drafting room and the dining room. The stage in our theater had to be enlarged to accommodate more musicians and musical instruments. We are always at full pitch, sawing, soldering, and concrete-mixing. Our activities never cease.

We also had to build more tents. Sixty white shepherd tents are scattered throughout the desert. They occupy the northwest position in relation to the camp buildings, and Iovanna refers to that section as "tent town."

It is beautiful. The young people have built smooth paths and concrete steps up and down the washes. They take tremendous pride in their tents.

Myra and Mark Heyman who were then married just a short time took me to view the site for their tent. We walked up the twisting path, narrowly escaping cruel cholla, staghorn and prickly pear cactus, until we came to the foot of the mountain. They showed me the palo verde tree that would almost touch their tent. Mark had already made his design which Mr. Wright had approved. It was interesting to see Myra, a young woman from New York City, fall in love with desert life and the adventure of living in a picturesque tent.

The boys have their locker rooms on one side of the camp; and on the other the girls have a luxurious new powder room with wardrobe closets, cabinets, showers and so on.

Life in the desert is an adventure. The boys have

built and are adding more concrete platforms with outside fireplaces, and terraces leading to their tents, having no limitation of space or imagination except for a certain allotment of materials to which they have access. Some of the tents are of extraordinary beauty. The boys learn to depend entirely upon the skill of their work because many a tent has blown down on their heads during the night. When the Desert Devil—the wind—encircles their tent, bringing it down around them, they have to extricate themselves in the middle of the night.

One boy could not part with the comfort of his former environment. He bought an air-mattress and a sleeping bag filled with down. One night a strong wind blew and tore his tent off its mooring from one side and threw it over the palo verde tree on the other side. And when this young son of an aristocratic family found himself in the embrace of the desert wind and wilderness, he jumped up to retrieve his tent. Meanwhile the wind lifted his light down sleeping bag and the air mattress and rolled them along the desert for hundreds of feet. He searched for them all night, a lantern in hand, only to find the mattress hanging over a cholla, punctured; and the sleeping bag far away, torn by cactus needles.

From that night on he firmly secured the ropes of his tent. It never blew away again. The young man had been told many times that his tent was fastened too carelessly—he had not believed anyone. It seems our share to learn only by experience. Having learned the bitter lesson, he gave up the idea of sleeping on an air mattress. After three winters in the desert, he knew everything about life in it and was hopefully warning others who also did not listen, and who in turn learned by experience.

Our young people take great pride in maintaining their tents neatly and beautifully. Around them they plant flowers or desert shrubs, which they transplant from the further parts of the desert. They build fireplaces and one can often see the fires at night glowing softly and one hears the young voices, sometimes singing old songs of the desert. Sometimes one can hear them late at night hammering and sawing in their tents, carrying out new ideas. The sounds of musical instruments too—flute, guitar and cello—flood the desert after sunset.

They often invited Mr. Wright and me for tea or to have steaks for supper, broiled over their fireplaces. On the trees and shrubs close by, they hung lanterns they themselves had made. Sometimes they played Mexican or Western music and often sang for us just before we were leaving. While filing down the narrow desert paths back to our camp, we could still hear them.

There are many hardships in the desert. The temperature sometimes falls as low as seventeen degrees above zero. In that cold weather, both Mr. Wright and I had slept outside in our sleeping bags. There are just two difficult periods—one, going into the sleeping bag at night, and the other, getting out of it in the morning. Both periods are sharp and severe but they last only a few minutes. After that we quickly adjusted ourselves.

In recent years we have lived more luxuriously in

real rooms! I always thought my room especially beautiful, with a closed-in patio adjoining it. Along the walls grow brilliant red bougainvillaea. They hang low over the round moongate. In front of my concrete terrace sweet alyssum is perpetually in full bloom and its fragrance reaches into my room. I have a small pool about twelve feet by fifteen feet enclosed by three high stone walls. Over them rise the bamboo grove, oleander trees and one tall saguaro cactus. Far in the distance is the outline of Superstition Mountain.

Our first Sunday breakfast in our newly enlarged and modified dining room was a pleasant experience to us all. Since interior decorating at Taliesin has always been taught in practice, Mr. Wright freely criticized every new arrangement of the tables, chairs, tablecloths, flower decorations, etc., made weekly by our young people. When some arrangement was particularly good, Mr. Wright described at length to the gathering why it was good.

On this morning Mr. Wright and I were so blinded by the light that we could see only the outlines of the people. So Mr. Wright began his usual Sunday morning address with the following words:

"I think you are so lucky not facing the light . . . that is a very bad proposition architecturally. I hope it will all sink into you. Never design houses where people have to sit facing the light. If you are sideways you can turn your head and see. And that is the best way. That is the way it should be. That is the beauty of the triangle. You can do this—you always sit sideways to

the center. Lay it out on paper some time and you will
see it.

"Well, what do all of you want to talk about this
morning?" he continued. "There are a lot of you here
now. I'm not accustomed to being in such a large company! Pretty hard to cover you all, but you are all here
with practically the same intent. And from very different angles, no doubt, and very different sources of
inspiration.

"Because all of you are inspired, aren't you? Inspired
by what, when, or how, that is the question. But inspired you all are with some desire, some intent, some
deepfelt wish, which is a prayer, you know. A prayer
is nothing but a deepfelt wish. And I think a prayer
should always be silent, and probably mostly is. What
you're praying for most, you know best, and yet I've
been surprised frequently by boys who really had a
deepfelt wish and were unaware of it. They were mostly
the ones who had been educated. They had been taught
a prayer or the equivalent of one which they would
recite while feeling something else entirely. I hope that
is not true of any of you. Because I cannot think of a
state more detrimental to the ambition of the young
architect than to straddle the fence like that. To have
deep in his heart one wish and to have to conform to
the conditions and demands of another—that is what
makes a bad marriage and will also make a bad architect. You have to go wholeheartedly into anything in
order to achieve that which is worth having. And if
your allegiance is divided, if your thought is divided,
if your feeling is confused . . . get rid of that condition
as soon as you can.

"Really to believe in something is the greatest boon, I think, and to believe wholeheartedly in it and to serve it with all your strength and your might—that is salvation. And in this day it is so hard to come by and so few people ever arrive at it that it is almost negligible, certainly in educational circles. Because I think in the higher educational circles they are presented with so many confusing thoughts and ideas that there is no clear one for them to drink when they finish their course. They are full of dregs like a wine that is not fit to drink.

"Anybody with personal experience, anyone who has been through the mill, has discovered the things we have been talking about to be true. I never liked that saying of Pilate's, 'Truth, what is truth?' The answer to that is simple, very simple . . . what is natural. Now then comes the question, what is nature and natural? It would be organic, of course. And organic is a good word to use in connection with that ideal you are seeking.

"Let us take up that word this morning and thresh it out. What is 'organic'? What would be organic? Of course, something hanging in the butcher shop is organic; a dead carcass of a pig, or a live one too, for that matter, is organic. But there is another phase, another sense to this term organic. And that is what is profoundly interrelated—one thing to another, consistent as a whole. That is organic in the sense we use it. So when I say that architecture is organic, I mean the whole is to the part as the part is to the whole. It is consistently one thing, especially for the purpose for which it was designed. That ties you down pretty flat and it is pretty hard to get away from it. And when it really possesses you and really gets hold of you, you are on the road to doing something good. Now it may not seem good to your neighbors, it may not seem good to the man next to you, but if it is good to you in that sense, it will prove to be good in the course of time. My own experience is bearing that out for your benefit. I started with this some sixty-five years ago and it is growing better and better and stronger and stronger all over the world ever since. Why? Because it is according to the laws and principles of what is natural. Now, of course, artificiality can be carried so far, and is carried so far by us, that it *seems* the natural thing. There is our difficulty in culture, in education—in being able to distinguish, to discriminate, between what is our natural state and what it is that has been foisted upon us by education—artificiality all down the line.

"Now to be natural doesn't mean to be a savage. To be natural doesn't mean to be crude. To be natural simply means to know which is right side up and which is wrong side up. And to have it in your hearts as an inheritance from, well . . . let us say, on high, or from somewhere where we all came from, that justifies your thought to you. And there you are with the possession of something precious to defend which is your own conviction. Now you can be wrong, of course. Many of the most 'convictious' persons in the world have been deadly wrong. There was Hitler, for instance, and a great many examples that you could name . . . people who felt that they were right, but who were absolutely wrong.

"But in all of us there is a quality, a little something,

I think it is referred to as 'a still small voice.' I have heard that all my life. 'Listen to the still small voice of conscience.' Now a man's conscience is really the mainspring of his soul. So listen attentively to conscience, always. Freedom without it is dangerous. Your conscience is your guiding star and the finest thing about you in principle where manhood or womanhood is concerned. That is putting it in terms of organic architecture. Now the good building of good design is the design that squares up with what I have just defined as a good conscience . . . where the materials you use are understood and lovingly and correctly used as materials. Where the design you make has in it the properties of truth—and that means the design that is appropriate and square for the purpose for which it was intended. You know why the shape of a thing is that shape and you know where to quit and how far to go with it and how far not to go, but that is something that will take you a long term of years to be really sure that you know. That is the most difficult thing to face as young architects.

"A sense of proportion is a conscientious realization of limitation. That is a good definition and you will not find it in a dictionary. For the designer, good conscience is the fruit of much serious devotion, study and experience. All you can expect of young fellows in that connection is a desire, a feeling that they want the best, the highest and the truest, and being willing to make sacrifices to get it. That is where it is first manifest. Then it grows and grows and grows, until after a while the very thing you do and the very thing you see becomes more and more the thing that you are—a

conscientious liberation in terms of human feeling—
or how you live, what you live in, what you live for. In
other words, architecture.

"Architecture by innate sense of the things we are
talking about—nowhere in the world, I believe, has
been specifically laid out in terms of accomplishment.
It has had all sorts of names: there was the Gothic,
which we would say came close, not too close; Byzantine, closer; and the Oriental Gothics; Persian, probably the closest of all. Then comes Chinese architecture,
native, characteristic, brother of the pine, the pine
tree that is the original of the Chinese temple.

"And so, out of environment, out of all that surrounds
the human being, he derives a certain strength of
imagery, of imagination, and he cannot get at the
sound that comes from the drum by cutting out the
head of it. That is what education has been trying to do
all these years.

"But what he can do is study the nature of his environment. An architect can study the nature of whatever attracts his attention. And as I have so often told,
he can soon accumulate or get the practice of looking
into the thing instead of just *at* it. And looking *in* he
will always see these relationships that will appeal to
his artist-conscience. His artistic conscience will gradually develop and save him from being foolish and save
him from betraying his clients and save him from adding to the errors which now disgrace the country and
the whole world. When you apply this test of thought
and of deep feeling you will realize what is being done
in the name of architecture.

"All this is religious. Yes, all this is square with true

religion, not with sectarianism. And all this is true, square with science. But science represents the lower forms, the lower strata, the physical means only. And of course we—not having very great contact with the things of the spirit of which we are talking nor with the depths of being, which really is the same thing—are too quickly enamoured by science. We have been of course overloaded and pushed to the brink of destruction by our devotion to science and our inability to understand what we have left out by way of art, architecture, and religion. Now, there is no architecture that is not religious. There is no feeling of the artist independent of religion.

"Religion has many definitions and comes in many packages; as many almost as the stuff you see in the market. And it is the confusion of thought and confusion in our lives that renders nearly everything we do commonplace, ineffective, and perhaps a little of this or a little of that, but nothing really fine, noble and convincing as a whole. So in order to get this thing into your systems, you have to have a feeling toward it that is really religious. I am sure that if there is a definition of religion that is really sound and true it means just the things I have been talking about now. And to refer to it as a sectarian affair is, of course, to refer to our weakness. To talk of beauty as one thing and to talk of, say, Unitarianism as another is all a blind floundering around to try to get to the core of Truth which is so simple that they won't take it. It is not good enough; it will not support all these divisions and various processions in the direction of something or other, somewhere, somehow, sometime.

"So the architect must be master in interior sense not only of his tools, not only of his materials, but of the human spirit. The soul of humanity is in his charge really. If that civilization to which he belongs is to endure long upon the face of the earth he must eventually realize that architecture is to him his religion. But now that, of course, seems high-falutin' and takes you far afield from where you want to go. Most of you will hire as men for other architects for a while, and then you will build something for yourselves. But I believe if you take this thing seriously enough and take it to heart and really get that feeling for it into your systems, you will emerge. It may take time, some time, years perhaps, but eventually you will produce something invaluable to your race and to your kind.

"So, do not let it bother you if they say that you are making a religion out of architecture—because you are, and you should. And the more you do, the better will be the architecture. But after all, the main thing about it is that you will be so much better. What it will do for you is something tremendous. To have a cause and a loyalty at heart for a cause that is deep and profound will make your sense of yourself as a man—will give your manhood a fine . . . I was going to say, refuge, because you will need it oftentimes, but a fine stance. You will be square on your spiritual feet and they cannot push you around.

"This has been a little sermon this morning and I apologize but it was coming to you and now you have had it. So let us now go on and walk over the hills and see what is over the mountain there on the other side. How many of you are capable of getting over on the other side? Over there is something beautiful. When I was a boy I read a book called Arney, Arney Sol Bakken. It was a little book. Arney was always wondering what was over there, over the mountains. Arney could not sleep for what was over the mountains, until one day in spite of everything and everybody, he packed up, put a knapsack on his back, and started out to go over there. And Arney never came back and nobody ever knew what he found."

We had barely settled in the desert when a giant plane took us to San Francisco. It was just before Christmas, and flying toward the city at night with its beautifully scattered light patterns was exciting to all the passengers—our faces were fastened to the windows.

"San Francisco looks almost more interesting at night than New York," I said.

"This is a greater city than New York," Mr. Wright said. "It is more independent, freer from the European influence. New York is really a fringe of London. I hope that San Francisco does not begin to ape New York with its conglomeration of citizenry, skyscrapers and chase for profit. Life in San Francisco is more flexible, more at ease, because industry and agronomy are well synchronized. The contact of long years with the Oriental nations has taught the people the value of the land and the emphasis on beauty, as well as profit in developing it."

The next morning I walked up and down its colorful steep streets. Streetcars still run on the rails and the cables, their bells ringing, as I used to hear them many years ago in cities of Europe. San Francisco does seem to be apart from other cities in the United States. It is under the influence of both the West and the Orient. The salespeople are eager to please; the general atmosphere is that of friendliness. And, of course, the many Japanese, Chinese, Korean, Philippine and Hawaiian faces give it a cosmopolitan air.

I asked Aaron Green, our former apprentice and now representative of the Frank Lloyd Wright Foundation in San Francisco, about the cultural development of the city.

"People are divided into two groups," he answered. "The aristocratic strata, with a conservative, sound cultural basis, have for years contributed to the artistic world of our city. The other group consists of the younger, smarter, more sophisticated and somewhat bohemian-inclined generation. They, too, have influenced our cultural trend. The two, I would say, harmonize well in promoting the best in the arts, music and literature."

Chapter 3

TALIESIN NORTH—WISCONSIN

Horses have long been a steady part of our Taliesin life. Many years ago when our children, Svetlana and Iovanna, were very young, Mr. Wright and I took them to buy horses from a farmer in a nearby valley.

Svetlana chose Pepper, a western horse, branded, amiable of countenance. Svetlana was happy with her horse.

Iovanna went wild with joy over her little black round-bellied Shetland pony. Her name was Blackie, a perfectly fitting name for that little devil.

White Beauty was for me—a plump self-assured animal who looked at me with liquid mellow eyes. When I said to the owner that I did not know much about horses, he answered, "Why, Mrs. Wright, this is the most gentle mare in the whole state of Wisconsin! Five or six kids at a time climb on her and she is always very good to them."

I was delighted. Maybe at last I could enjoy a horse without fear.

Mr. Wright already had Trixie, a tall, aristocratic, five-gaited horse. Her snobbish manner inspired fear in me—I did not dare ride her.

We frequently rode down our back road and across the pasture to the hill we call Phoebe Point. Mr. Wright always headed the line, the three of us following. I am sure that all the horses respected Mr. Wright as the master because they behaved beautifully when he was with us.

Little by little I became more relaxed and accustomed to White Beauty. I cleaned her stall, brushed her and fed her. One day I was feeding her corn which she ate with greedy gusto, occasionally turning her head to look at me with those moist eyes of hers. I came close and petted her flanks. All of a sudden she gave me such a swift and potent side kick in the upper half of my leg that it took me off my feet and laid me out for two weeks!

I complained bitterly to Mr. Wright that horses must be like human beings; after a month or so they begin to show their real nature. "That man has not told us the truth about White Beauty," I insisted.

"Of course he told the truth," Mr. Wright said. "But don't you see your error? You gave her only one ear of corn—she expected another. Instead of feeding her you petted her. Naturally she became irritated and kicked."

That was always my experience with Mr. Wright—a horse could do no wrong. I learned to be more cautious and at the same time more daring. Since Beauty was a horse that also could be hitched to a buggy, I used to drive her all over the countryside. One day I drove her past our little chapel and up the winding roads into the hills. As usual, with no visible cause, Beauty decided to kick up her hind legs, jiggling me and the buggy up and down the grade. I tried to get her to go faster hoping to snap her out of it—that did not help. I tried to hold her in and stop her—that did not help. Somehow or other, we wretchedly returned to Taliesin. I complained to Mr. Wright, "This horse is terrible. She gave me such trouble on the road."

"Why," he said, "it must have been something you did to provoke her. Why should she have given you any trouble?"

"I don't understand why. I tried every means to stop her from balking."

"Well," he said, "you simply should have paid no attention to her and held steady on to her reins. When a horse constantly gets pulled in or let out, she naturally gets fidgety. You should have let her alone and she would have calmed down."

Another time when Mr. Wright and I were returning from a picnic, Beauty balked and kicked and our buggy went from one side of the road to the other with her tricky jumps. I was hanging on to the buggy and to Mr. Wright, pleading with him, "Please, let's stop. Let us get out. Can you stop her? Did I not tell you she was tricky?"

"Nonsense," he said, "she will calm down." With an unconcerned expression on his face, he let that horse balk and kick for a short while and then, to my surprise, she resumed her trotting gait.

"What is the matter with this horse?" I asked.

"Nothing," he said quietly. "All that is the matter with her is that she wants to go home faster than her gait permits. She gets angry with herself about it and kicks. She doesn't mean anything bad by it."

A year later we acquired another horse. The name of

this little brown beast was Queen. She, too, looked docile and the man who sold her also told us that "she was as gentle as a lamb and that all the kids piled up on her and she just would not hurt them for the world!"

Almost a month after we acquired Queen I headed down the road for a short afternoon ride. She had been perfectly fine that month. But on this particular afternoon when we approached the bridge below Taliesin, Queen made a most unexpected swift turn and breaking into a fast gallop she took me back up the hill, swerved around the curve, through the gate, through the back court, into the stable and directly into her stall! This was very humiliating but fortunately no one had seen me. I tried to get her out but she would not move and gave me one of those evil horse looks . . . I had to get off and lead her out.

Mr. Wright had told me that I must never have a horse win over me. So, discouraged as I was, I took her back to the bridge and we stayed at that bridge for about fifteen minutes. She balked and twisted her body around like a snake, but I hung on—and at last we crossed.

From then on for some time whenever we encountered a bridge, we fought each other but eventually Queen crossed bridges without resistance. I was determined to become a good horsewoman. I wanted to be a fit riding companion to Mr. Wright.

One morning Iovanna, riding Blackie and I, Queen, saw our neighbor, John Michels, in his garden. We stopped and chatted with him for a while. On bidding us good-bye John went into the barn. I started ahead on Queen but Blackie would not move. As though molded of iron, the creature stood immobile, pressing her front legs into the ground. Iovanna burst into tears.

I rode back and called John for help. He laughed at our ridiculous plight, then backed up several yards, ran fast toward Blackie and kicked her so hard that she shot out like a round little baseball—and rolled onto the highway without stopping. I could hardly catch up— Blackie could go very fast.

We rode up a shady hill where the wild grapes swung their vines over the fences, where blackberries were to be found, where wild choke cherries grew. We did not realize until we had almost reached the top of the hill that it was far past lunchtime.

"Let us go back," I said. "It's late."

But Blackie did not feel like going back. She liked it on the hill and stood staring in front of her with that familiar dark look. I went around her trying to give a push. No use. And being on a steep slope I did not dare dismount since I was not sure that I could remount because Queen always performed a dance whenever I tried to get on. I am sure she did this in the hope of exhausting my strength.

We stayed on the slope of that hill for half an hour, while Iovanna bawled and Blackie angrily whipped her tail, quivering her vicious little black nostrils. Strong of character, moody, evil of nature, Blackie cared for nothing except her moods. And she had plenty of them. She fell into her moods as often as she pleased. From that day on we did exactly what Blackie wanted.

Early one morning I saddled Queen, and Iovanna, at the age of six, very deftly saddled her Blackie. We rode to the division of the road where our Triangle garden is now and, being ahead, I turned right. But Blackie had a different idea; she simply turned left. And that was all—I could do nothing. So I turned left to follow Blackie where she wanted to go. And once more Iovanna burst into tears. "Mother, you know what I am going to do when I die? I am going to haunt Blackie," she sobbed.

"Blackie is a Shetland pony, Iovanna. I have heard that the Shetland pony is obstinate and it is not up to you to mold her or change her. It won't do you any good to haunt her rusty little wicked soul . . . It is all right that we turned left. It is just as nice on this side of the hill as on the other," I pretended. I knew too well the profound humiliation for me to have to follow that little black monster wherever her whim took her.

This struggle with Blackie lasted for several years, and I must say I was happy when we got rid of her.

Iovanna was now big enough to ride a horse. For twenty-five dollars we bought a horse named Jeppo. He had light blonde hair and a light beige mane and tail. Iovanna was happy with Jeppo and, after years of having to contend with Blackie's demoniacal nature, believed him to be an angel. She could do whatever she wanted with him. Perhaps the experience with dark-souled Blackie was good because Iovanna became as fine a horsewoman as can be found anywhere. She could make a horse do anything she pleased. In later years Iovanna, like her father, always explained to me why my horse did this or that. Horses always were to me inscrutable, detached beings of whom I understood not a particle. Every horse was a new enigma.

I did graduate to riding Mr. Wright's Trixie, however, with a certain amount of ease. I was riding up the steep Taliesin hill on her back late one morning. I was pleased that she gave me no trouble. Enjoying my ride, I leaned down over Trixie's head to pet her when she jerked her head back and hit me in the middle of my forehead—with such force that I almost fell off. I barely managed to cling to the saddle. By the time we reached the stable I had a great big bump that later spread black and blue all over my face. At luncheon I complained about it to Mr. Wright and Iovanna. Iovanna spoke up unhesitatingly, "You should never have done that! Don't you see that she was happy going home, she didn't want to be bothered by you?"

"Was that so?" I said. "Oh, so that is it. She just simply didn't want even to be touched!"

"No, you should not have petted her then. A horse knows when she is being praised for something. There was nothing to praise her for."

"You should have let her alone," said Mr. Wright. "Mother, the trouble with you is that you simply don't know when you are well off on a horse. You have to learn to let well enough alone . . ."

I never heard him once say a bad word about a horse! He knew their psychology, their state of mind, and their state of being. He knew the horse as he knew nature and there was a perfect master-horse relationship between them. The horse always gave in to his wishes—with no strain or pressure on his part.

Svetlana had no trouble whatsoever with her Pepper. Somehow the temperament of Pepper and the temperament of Svetlana blended so beautifully they always had a good time with each other wherever they went. There did not seem to be any necessity of a master and horse relationship. The two of them were friends. Svetlana went on her Pepper, jogging along on the western saddle at Pepper's own crisp trot, lope or gallop which they enjoyed in silent agreement. There never was a quarrel between them—the struggle for mastery was entirely absent. It was a long and lasting friendship. Pepper with his gentle spirit lived long after Svetlana left us.

Mysterious, wild-eyed, queer creatures, horses remain for me. I realize that their world and mine have nothing in common and that never will I be able to have the kind of communion with a horse that my family enjoyed. Horses are not part of my world. But since it is my gospel to overcome all obstacles, I became quite an experienced horsewoman.

After I had been asking Mr. Wright for a long time to let me learn to drive a car, he finally yielded and bought a Model A Ford for me. That was thirty-two years ago. Our mason, the late Philip Volk, drove me down to the field below Taliesin to show me the mysteries of the machine. After about half an hour of instruction, he let me drive up the hill for the very first time. That same afternoon I asked Mr. Wright if it would be all right for me to try driving the Ford by myself.

"You cannot keep away from it, can you?" he said smiling. "Do you know how to stop?"

"Yes," I answered gladly.

"Go ahead then. Go slowly and I will walk along."

68

Once at the wheel I was so excited that I mixed the gears, but somehow got myself straightened out—and we went. Mr. Wright urged me to shift more often so that I could learn more quickly. He walked by the side of the road, asking me to make frequent stops. The hill was steep and I jerked the car a great deal. At one point I went ahead, and shifted to high gear, feeling that I was doing quite well. When down at the flat part of the road Mr. Wright said, "Back up now," I turned the steering wheel and "backed." But what I really did was to shift into second instead of reverse and that shot me square against the stone culvert, smashing the right fender.

"What are you doing?" Mr. Wright said exasperatedly. "I told you to back up."

At this point my knowledge of the machine had come to an end. Whatever I did, whichever way I shifted, I found myself always in second gear. The reverse had simply vanished. Still making useless attempts to look for it, I kept pushing worse than before against the culvert.

"You are going to ruin this car and push the wall down besides!" Mr. Wright spoke impatiently. "Cut that out! I told you to back up!" And he motioned with his hand.

I sat at the wheel in a rage at myself. "I cannot find the reverse," I said. "It has disappeared. Maybe I did something that made it go out."

"Disappeared! Come out of that car. Let us walk up," he waved his hand. And as we walked up the Taliesin hill he said kindly, "I should not have let you drive after the first lesson. We will send somebody down for the car."

During that week I drove at every spare moment, unfortunately smashing all the fenders but one. I believed that this was due to the limited space of our back court in which I was practicing by myself. At last one day I drove down on the highway, just to the mailbox and back. At the end of the week our friend Dr. Blount came to visit us.

"Would you like to drive down with me to the mailbox?" I asked her.

"I would love to," she answered.

On the way down I drove very well, even better than I thought I would. At the mailbox I had to use the reverse to turn around, and suddenly this gear vanished again. Finding myself forever in second, I almost knocked the mailbox down. Dr. Blount said nothing, but pushed her body back and braced her feet against the floor of the car every time I drove forward.

"Something got stuck," I said, appearing unconcerned—and at that very moment I slipped into reverse, not knowing how it happened. We turned around and off we headed toward Taliesin.

"How long have you been driving?" Dr. Blount asked quietly.

"One week today," I said proudly.

Something happened to Dr. Blount. She stiffened up, clutched the handle of the car door, stared intently in front of her, moving her body with every curve I made. This made me lose whatever confidence I might have had. Three times, trying to get up the steep Taliesin back road, I killed the engine and rolled back all the

Entrances: Above, Taliesin West, Arizona; and Taliesin, Wisconsin.

Mrs. Wright and Trixie.

In the Lectracar-Surrey.

Mr. Wright and his favorite horse, Johnny Walker.

way down to the bridge on the highway. And finally, the fourth time, without shifting from third gear and with the radiator boiling full steam, I roared up to the Taliesin steps where Mr. Wright was standing, waiting.

"I thought so," he said. "She took you to the mailbox. She takes any chance for an excuse to drive the car. Olgivanna is just learning."

"I found that out," Dr. Blount smiled with a sigh of relief. I did not ask her to go with me again, and she never asked me either.

I learned how to drive the car. How many times in years past, driving back and forth between Wisconsin and Arizona, Mr. Wright urged me to pass cars on the roads.

"Eat him up," he would say. "Go ahead—eat him up." And I would step on the gas and fly in our powerful cars past Cadillacs, Buicks, Studebakers, Dodges, at top speeds—leaving them all behind diminishing on the long ribbons of the highways.

He taught me all the fine points a good driver should possess. He was a strict teacher, but a very fine one. He himself was a fast driver, but I never met a better one. His superb correlation made beautiful everything he did with accuracy, grace and ease.

In order to keep our apprentices from spending weekend evenings in aimless entertainment, we have always endeavored to give them a cultural basis for growth through various mediums: music, the dance, drama and motion pictures. Good films are of course scarce and we have had some poor ones. However, since learning goes on every moment, we keep learning and we hope that someday we will find a magic source from which we can consistently draw the best of the moving pictures that can be had in the world.

From the very first years of the Taliesin Fellowship, Mr. Wright and I put some of the more responsible of our young people in charge of various departments of work. One such department was, and still is, in the hands of Eugene Masselink, now the Secretary and Treasurer of the Frank Lloyd Wright Foundation. He books films on the basis of his wide reading or on the recommendations of friends. He can rarely know before the showing what the film will be like; and every now and then, notwithstanding praise or fine reviews, somehow or other we receive a poor film. Of course he usually pays for his errors. In the past when he would see Mr. Wright and me grow restless in our chairs, realizing that the film was a mediocre one, he would quietly disappear. "I always feel as though I had conceived, produced and acted that play," he would complain.

About twenty-five years ago, Gene booked an "art film" believing it to be educational and aesthetically produced as an "art film" is supposed to be. The name of the film was *Pandora's Box*, a German production, and since many believed that films coming from Europe were almost always bound to be distinguished we had no doubt that we were going to see a beautiful film.

Mr. Wright and I decided to share the pleasure of this film with our neighbors, so we invited some Wisconsin friends—farmers and their wives—from nearby and, without seeing the film in advance, we presented it after dinner.

As we sat watching the development of this incredible motion picture I began to feel more and more uncomfortable. It was a cynical exposition of the experiences of many characters, all disagreeable, including Pandora herself. I whispered to Mr. Wright, "Please stop this film. Let us apologize and tell them we did not know what it was."

"No, don't do that," Mr. Wright answered. "We would disappoint our friends. After all we don't know—it might turn out to be all right. Perhaps it is just this part that isn't good."

The film continued to unreel in an absolute disregard for beauty, violating all values. "Why was this called an 'art film?'" I thought resentfully. I looked around at our audience. They were all possessed by the kind of fascination that comes with something unheard of, something never seen or experienced before—the eyes of our audience were glued to the screen!

Again I whispered to Mr. Wright, "Please, let us get out of here. I cannot face these people. What will they think of us?"

"Never mind," he said. "The Germans have good movie directors—it might get better."

Forever an optimist he was. We sat through the entire devastating, dull, dreary, uninteresting exposition of a woman who went from bad to worse. The technique was poor, the acting was coarse. But not one of our audience moved, and I whispered to Mr. Wright, "They are not leaving because they are afraid to offend us. If you and I go, I am sure they will go too."

75

"No," he said. "You are going to stay right where you are. It will be offensive to them. Let us find something good in this experience."

"Oh, goodness," I thought in anguish, waiting for the dreadful thing to end.

Finally the torture was over. Mr. Wright got up and said, "Too bad. We apologize to all of you. That's what happens to us when we don't know what a film is about. Where is Gene?" But Gene had of course left long ago.

Our guests were kind. "Well, it can't be helped," one said. And a more optimistic one said, "It was not too bad and maybe it was even instructive to see how queer things can sometimes get." And they thanked us most graciously!

Some years ago when Mr. Wright and I went to Chicago, we were driven by John Howe who is now one of the Taliesin Associated Architects. As Mr. Wright had a business appointment on that very hot day, Jack and I while waiting for him went to a cool theater on Michigan Avenue. They were showing Emile Zola's *Nana* with Anna Sten, a new actress at that time, and we were pleased with the film.

Upon returning to Taliesin I recommended it for one of our Saturday showings. However, when presented in our Playhouse, *Nana* inexplicably underwent a shocking metamorphosis. It lost all the charm it had had in the Chicago theater! It was a bitter lesson to learn how impressions change with time and circumstances, so I no longer speak of any picture with certainty but with a hesitance which might give me some way of justifying myself.

76

When our apprentices enjoy a movie in Chicago, Madison, New York or wherever they happen to stop around the country, they often recommend it to us enthusiastically. Sooner or later the film is shown in our Playhouse and if the criticism rises to a high volume the apprentice who suggested it rises from his seat and vanishes—branded and teased for years for his poor taste. It is hard at Taliesin to live down a bad film!

Arnold Roy once recommended a satire which delighted us all. Then, encouraged by such success, Arnold suggested *Once Upon a Horse:* "One of the funniest comedies Bruce Pfeiffer and I have ever seen," he laughed. We sent for the film. It was frightful, a low slapstick parody on the American Western, and practically all of the audience walked out. Poor Arnold and Bruce—they have not heard the last of it yet.

But people are good-natured about such mishaps; fortunately they do not occur frequently. We pride ourselves on having shown the finest American and foreign films produced in the last thirty years. We often go back to our old favorites and, besides enjoying their artistry and technique, we like to reminisce about the events that surrounded the viewing of each of them in the past. And for the new apprentices it is a fresh and welcome experience.

Years ago we went to the Madison Union Theater one night, taking some twenty members of the Fellowship with us to see the film *Congress Dances* which starred Lillian Harvey, the European actress, whom Mr. Wright greatly admired. As we all sat down, Mr. Wright stood up and announced loudly, "Boys, she's not yours, she's mine!" This upset me terribly. Mr. Wright liked Lillian Harvey too much, I thought. "I know she is a wonderful and charming actress, but don't you think you're going too far?" This made no difference.

I was just about getting over Lillian Harvey when Marlene Dietrich came along. It was then that I really burned with jealousy. I suffered with it so many times that it was finally all burned out of me: I had to see her in *Flame of New Orleans* endless times. "Look here," I said to Mr. Wright, "here you are enjoying yourself while I sit and watch you—I am going to find some actor that I can like as much as you like Marlene Dietrich."

But I never could. Charles Boyer impressed me for a while, but Mr. Wright fixed that. We saw him in a picture with Irene Dunne. I did think that Charles Boyer was good in it, so I had the lack of wisdom to mention this a couple of times the next day. "Well," he said, "you *would* like somebody like that!" And then he proceeded to destroy him with faultless method.

It started on a trip to Madison. All the way into town, to everything I said, he answered in an elaborate manner with an exaggerated French accent. At first I was amused and then it began to get me. "Enough is enough!" I said. "You are rubbing it in too hard. I understand. I get the point."

"Oh? Thees does not pleeze Madame?"

"If you don't stop, I'm going to open the door of this car and jump out."

"Oh, that is very fool-*eesh*! Oh, Madame, so very fool-*eesh*! You should ne-vair reesk your pre-cious li-ife."

78

"Stop," I said. "I won't take this any longer."

"Mais, Madame, I am so hap-pee you like such magnifique man—like Monsieur Boyer. Mais oui, oui, oui . . . tres bon, tres magnifique!"

I grabbed one handle of the car, "Stop or I'll jump!"

During lunch he continued, "Moth-aire, a leetle sugaire?"

Mr. Wright fixed Charles Boyer forever. After that whenever I saw him in pictures all I could think of was Mr. Wright. Charles Boyer's manner of speech and accent sounded so completely artificial to me that I wanted to laugh even when the dialogue was serious.

On the other hand, I never could destroy Marlene Dietrich for Mr. Wright. I simply did not know how, that's all. She won. Charles Boyer lost.

After that experience if I thought even slightly well of some actor I kept it to myself if I wanted to enjoy his acting for any length of time—Mr. Wright's reactions had a powerful effect on me.

We both admired his granddaughter, Anne Baxter. He was very proud of her, and we would drive for miles to see her in films. "She is a great actress," he said. "Anne does beautiful work: I have never once seen her fail to portray a character to perfection."

We had little trouble in agreeing about moving pictures except that I did not like seeing them over and over again. He saw *The Ghost Goes West* some ten or twelve times. He told us when he once went to see it in New York he laughed from beginning to end and at the end of the picture a man behind him leaned over and said, "I certainly enjoyed hearing you enjoy yourself—more power to you!"

79

Often we would laugh together, Mr. Wright taking long pauses, tears of laughter rolling down his cheeks. "Oh, shucks! This is too funny for words. This is rich," he would manage to say while his laughter increased to a deep contagious pitch. The people in the theater would turn toward us laughing, too, or in a useless attempt to hush us . . .

That is the way he would laugh. I know of no one who can laugh with such deep pleasure, with such complete, beautiful abundance.

Laughter like that is rare. A simple, natural reaction to a funny situation is gradually being lost to us. We know only intellectualized laughter. Through excess of polished wit, which arouses in us reactions of a more processed nature, we no longer react with direct, natural spontaneity—the gusty quality of irresistible laughter.

We have always created at Taliesin conditions in which the physical body is submitted to hardships in order to strengthen it and make it a perfect vehicle for life; conditions in which feeling may grow, the intellect surpass the mind, and the spirit take unimpeded flight.

Mr. Wright and I would submit ourselves to the same rugged discipline. We would get up at six in the morning to walk to breakfast in the moonlight. Wisconsin's cold winter mornings were overcome by our will and determination to work. There have always been new building projects, alterations and repairs.

We have worked hard with our young people in the faith that the vision of our ideal first shared with them

80

would spread and influence the world. Only a few have understood and been willing to learn the gospel of work combined from within and without at the same time, but we have gone strongly, firmly, determined to build a world in which we could prove that a society can be based on merit.

Often on bitter cold afternoons we would get our carriages and horses to take the Fellowship on a picnic in the hills, meadows or on the edge of a forest. We would build a large fire around which we stamped our feet, shivering from head to foot until we were warmed by the blaze. We would each grill our own steaks; potatoes were simply thrown into the fire to bake a hard black crust on them that they might keep their flavor. And the delicious coffee with Taliesin's own spice cake!

We would tell stories and anecdotes; sometimes Mr. Wright would speak of Gothic cathedrals, comparing them with a formation of rocks on the opposite side of the ravine—beautiful, natural, with the mystical quality of a cathedral.

Neither heat nor rain nor cold ever stopped us. We went on our weekly picnics and when the cars got stuck in the deep ruts of mud and our young people complained, "No use—we can't make it this time," Mr. Wright would come out of the car sinking in mud up to his ankles, his face illumined, enjoying every moment of fighting the obstacle.

"Push this way," he would call out, pointing with his cane. "You pull. You get in and steer."

"I cannot," the boy would resist.

"Yes, you can," he would answer and then everyone,

deep in the mud, pushed car after car, starting it and getting stuck again in the greasy, slippery ruts. His electrifying power was transmitted to them; everyone had bright red cheeks from the physical effort, the rain and the wind, laughing now, also enjoying the hardship.

All experiences are consumed into our inner structure to stay with us for life. The lightest efforts we make toward fighting transitory, negative experiences with an aim to rise above them—holding tight to the center rod within us—are paid back in abundant measure.

During long years of my life, I have often wondered at the emotional laziness which so many indulge in, contributing to its permanency by the use of various drugs. Why should people loathe to suffer in order to enter the gates of their own paradise? Why do they wish everything for nothing, be it in material or inner possessions? Sadness descended upon my spirit when I heard a student say one day, "My desire for striving toward a better life and undergoing interior discipline in order to get it is not strong enough. Much too often it leaves me."

The Zoroastrian idea of maintaining the eternal flame by taking fire from one to light another is a great symbol. The human being may be incapable of lighting his own spark. But after he has borrowed the flame from his neighbor and the fire within him has been lit, it is a criminal act, a violation of his spirit, if he fails to maintain the fire because of laziness. These dark blank spaces that I am forced to watch in those who have studied and worked with me are a grievance to me.

No one can maintain the flame of anyone else who is indulging in indolence. He must cherish the flame himself besides seeking those who can help him preserve it.

The prevailing emotional laziness is a great danger. Emotion is waning because the long years of school from kindergarten to college, spent in acquiring mere factual information, set the mind running on automatic tracks while the development of feeling is neglected, even ignored.

Through the strength of his belief in what constituted goodness and health, Mr. Wright possessed an electrifying power. In his long life he most often overcame sickness by ignoring it. He never pampered himself even when to all appearances it would seem to be a necessity. He endured pain, crushing through it and annihilating it; and he demanded the same of others. At times he appeared even ruthless.

Several years ago when I suffered paroxysms of tachycardia lasting from two to three hours or more, he looked after me tenderly. On one such occasion, just a few minutes after my attack was over he, feeling happy again, gave me his hand and said, "Mother, let us go on with the picnic we were planning. It will be good for you. Don't give in to sickness. You are all right now—come on, put on some colorful dress. Let us go."

"Please, wait," I pleaded. "Give me a little while to recover. I don't think it is good to get up right away."

"Oh, come on. You are strong in spirit. It will be good for you." He restlessly walked in and out of my room.

"Aren't you ready yet?" he asked impatiently while I started dressing with my hands trembling and my knees bending under me.

Then he put his strong arm around my waist, happy that I was up. He walked me to the car and we drove on to the picnic.

I have suffered these attacks for years, sometimes quite severely, and I disappointed him at times by not being able to get up as he always wanted me to. But in this, too, I believe that my final victory over the attacks came through his persistent demand, based on love and the wish to have me constantly by his side— and my wish to be with him. He helped to fix permanently within me physical endurance surmounting all barriers.

He had enormous esteem for his ancestral blood line and was partial to his Puritanical heritage. "The Puritans were good," he often said. "What would this country have been without the restraining effects of our Puritan forefathers?"

Puritanism was like a floating cell in his bloodstream, disappearing into the crevices of his being for a great length of time, but all of a sudden appearing again to take complete possession of him. He would become ascetic, straight as a steel rod. He would denounce alcohol, tobacco, coffee, tea, sweets, rouge, powder, lipstick, beauty parlors, jewelry, furs. He would suddenly strip life of all its rich clothing, of its living flesh, and righteously extol its fossilized morality. He would denounce love between men and women as mere sex. He would even denounce the birth of children! His whole countenance would suddenly undergo a complete change, his profile becoming sharp, thinly cut; the eyes narrowing into icy streaks, the lips tight, hard pressed—the image of a minister of the strictest ascetic denomination.

This fortunately never lasted long. The Puritanical blood cell disappeared as suddenly as it had appeared, and once again he was a free-thinker with vision and understanding of human passions.

However, one facet of his Puritanism stayed with him forever. He started smoking when he was about fifty and often declared, "I used the cigarette the way a darky uses a razor blade—for social purposes only." He never inhaled.

Many years ago, on one of our Saturday night social events at the Hillside theater, I noticed a grotesque silhouette of a young woman against the burning fireplace: in her mouth was a cigarette and with both her hands she was re-arranging her skirt, pulling it up at the waistline. It was an ugly sight.

I drew Mr. Wright's attention to it. "Isn't that an awful picture? It violates the beauty of this theater."

"Yes," he said, rather detached I thought. "Too bad." That was all.

But in the beginning of the very next week he issued a dictum to the members of the Taliesin Fellowship: not to smoke in the public rooms. Later he issued another dictum: not to smoke in their own rooms; they were permitted to smoke only out-of-doors. And then he no longer permitted them to smoke out-of-doors either.

And once when he found a package of cigarettes in

Kay Davison's car, he hurled them far out into the ravine, indignant at her affront.

"But can't they smoke when they take a trip in the car?" I asked.

"No," he said positively. "Smoking is a filthy habit."

From then on the smoking of a cigarette was the manifestation of sin. His Puritanical blood cell became fixed in relation to smoking.

Puritanism gave him joy in hardships—he thrived on difficulties. I remember our first summer together at Taliesin. He arranged a boat party for the late evening on our pond below the hill. That week end we had Lisa Glassenberg, a friend of mine, visiting us. I put on a light, white dress and aquamarine necklace he had given me. My friend wore a pale yellow gown made of dainty lace.

The mosquitoes were in full bloom. Over the delicate wooden frame that Mr. Wright himself had built above the boat he had hung a white mosquito netting, flowing in rich folds from all sides. Lighted Japanese lanterns of various colors were strung along the top of the framework.

We walked down to the wooden platform with gay anticipation and Mr. Wright, Lisa and I got into the boat which looked fantastically beautiful—ghostlike in the twilight. As he began rowing toward the upper bridge of the creek, a distance of a mile, we could hear the music of a Strauss waltz from the Taliesin hill. Our romantic boat glided to the beat of the oars and the rhythm of the music.

But the mosquitoes grew thicker. They were now a dark moving foam about us. The netting was coarse and starched, with openings wide enough for them to fly in without hindrance. Soon the dark mass outside the net filled the boat and we started a fight which we soon lost. The multitudes of winged little detestables attacked and freely drank blood from our lightly dressed bodies.

"We cannot go on like this! It is impossible. We must return. There is no use killing them—there are too many," I said.

But Mr. Wright with determination in his face and body kept rowing on—possessed. "Kill them, kill them. You will get them. Keep killing them," he repeated.

"We are already covered with welts. Let us turn back. We cannot continue like this. Please turn back!" I begged.

"Turn back?" he asked stunned. "We cannot turn back now! Kill them. Keep at it. We will get rid of them. Fight them—it won't hurt you to be bitten a little."

"A *little*? Look at us. Pretty soon I won't be able to see out of my eyes or breathe through my nose! Please turn back. This is a dreadful experience. Give it up."

"I will not," he said through clenched teeth and kept rowing upstream.

The music floated uselessly in the air as a background to the thin high-pitched voices of the flying black streaks.

"I did not know you were like this," he said. "How could you give up this beautiful occasion just because of a few bites? I worked on this boat all day so as to

87

give you pleasure. And you can't put up with a little hardship. Keep killing them."

I kept frantically waving my arms trying to protect my terrified friend as well as myself. Fury and despair were whirling inside me. I looked at his face—it was handsome and fearsome. His lower jaw was set. His Anglo-Saxon eyes slanted in burning steel and disdain.

I choked inside with indignation at his seemingly senseless abuse, and drew myself into silence. My friend was now crying. She leaned her head close to my ear and whispered, "Is he always like this?"

I looked at his green-streaked eyes and, lost in wonder and uncertainty, answered quietly, "I don't know . . ."

The silence became solid, uninterrupted in the boat except for my friend's occasional blowing of her nose. We kept going. My right eye was completely shut from the swelling. Mr. Wright rowed on and on all the way to the bridge, then, turning back, we continued our unhappy silent party until we landed at the platform. And when we stepped out, I tore past him in the dark, leaving my crying friend behind. "This is incredible— is it possible to build a life with a man like this?" I thought bewildered.

He came up to the house and sat in the chair opposite me, looking sad now with a soft smile on his lips and said, "I wanted to give you pleasure, don't you understand? It was a beautiful idea—I did not want it defeated. I thought we could fight off the mosquitoes. I am sorry to have hurt you."

"It is all right," I melted with tenderness. "I am

sorry I could not take it. But it was beautiful just the same."

"You're all right, Olgivanna," he said. "You stuck through it. We are made of strong metal; we should have an interesting life."

This was the first boulder which, instead of allowing it to destroy us, we built into our marriage.

The following spring we came across the second. One late afternoon we went for a walk, taking matches with us to burn the dry grass on the hill. I started lighting one section of the hill, and he another. The grass he lighted burned well and fast. The grass I lighted was green and I could not make it burn. I had already used up one box of matches and asked him for his. He came over, looked at the grass and said, "Don't bother with this part—it is too green—you cannot make it burn."

"But I can," I said. "All I need is more matches."

"All right," he said, "if you must learn by experience, go ahead."

I kept lighting matches laboriously, crawling on my knees, blowing with all my strength, trying to find some dry stems underneath the green. I used up all his matches and I could not make the grass burn.

"I told you," he said, "that grass is green—give it up."

"Please," I answered, "will you wait here while I run up to Taliesin to bring some more matches?"

"This is sheer nonsense," he said, irritated. "I did not know you were stubborn. It is not a good trait to have. Don't you see you cannot burn this grass?"

"But I found some dry stems, all I need is matches. Please wait for me."

"I am not going to stand here and watch this foolishness go on. When you are through with it, you will find me sitting on the stile up the hill."

I streaked up to Taliesin, snatched a box of matches, ran down fast and again tried to light the grass. I used up two-thirds of the new box, still crawling and blowing . . . I now had only a few matches left. I sprawled full length on the ground and pushing up on my hands, I blew from below. There at last I came across a large patch of dry stems hidden under the green. I kept blowing, determined not to give up. At last the little tongues of fire began to spread wider and wider, then gradually turned into flame that swept suddenly fast over the side of the hill.

"Come and look," I called. "The grass is burning!"

He came down, looked at the fire, and said incredulously, "I would not have believed it!"

And I stood triumphant over my own flames.

"I had better look out for you," he added, his face steeped in pleasure, his eyes gleaming. He took my arm, and walking close in the darkness, he said, "You are all right. You are my kind."

That was the second boulder built into our life. From then on he expected miracles of me and I of him. He never disappointed me.

Chapter 4

TALIESIN WEST—ARIZONA

I also remember one day in our Arizona camp when a deluge of rain came and the water gushed down the mountainside in torrents. Mr. Wright, Iovanna and I were each sitting in our compartments in the "Suntrap," which was our temporary shelter while the camp was being built. It consisted of three tiny independent structures big enough for a bed, bed stand and an adjoining closet. They faced an open concrete terrace with a fireplace in the corner.

Mr. Wright was playing a little organ, Iovanna was doing her homework, and I was reading Bucke's *Cosmic Consciousness,* my feet in four inches of water.

One of our young people, Herbert Fritz, ran up to the "Suntrap," pale and excited. We could hardly hear what he was saying. "All three of you should leave. It is dangerous for you to stay here—the water is rising higher every minute. Please," he pleaded, "you must drive into Phoenix and spend the night there."

He was right—the water was rising higher. We quickly got some night clothes together and, wading through the water, we managed to get to the car. As we drove down Shea Boulevard, a road of deep washes, ruts and rocks, we were stuck right in the middle of a wash with water up to our waists in the car! The thunder and lightning and the gushing, swift currents were frightening. But Mr. Wright was in his element—fighting the flood. He kept working the car with his body, never giving up the faith that it would start. It did.

We reached Phoenix and the house of our friend, Dr. Matanovich. With the help of his wife, Helen, we ran two tubfuls of hot water for Mr. Wright and Iovanna but I felt I was immune to catching a cold. The next day they were both well and bright, while I came down with the most vicious cold I had ever had in my life.

This kind of free attitude toward hardships weaves a strong spiritual fibre. It is harmful to our spirit to disassociate ourselves completely from the elements of nature. The force with which they press upon us we can equal by one which we exert upon them. The principle of all force is the same—as the forces of disaster and sorrow of life press against us, so we learn to measure our own to meet them.

I never saw him hesitate in decision. In the most serious situations of our lives he made swift decisions and between them and action there hardly ever was a pause. Decision and action were simultaneous—in his work as in his life.

When we went to Arizona for the building of the Arizona Biltmore Hotel, we fell in love with the desert and its magnificent mountains. "I wish we had a home in Arizona," I said. "This is such a different world from Wisconsin—like another planet. I imagine the moon must be something like Arizona—if it has sunshine."

"We will have a home in the desert," he said with assurance.

We were in terrible financial straits, barely making ends meet. Yet remembering that miracles happen to those that have faith I believed without doubt that before long we would have a home in this beautiful desert.

In the meantime we lived in a rented house in Phoenix. The town was small at that time. Arizona was just making its way toward an illustrious place on the United States map. The little house on Almeria Street in downtown Phoenix was hot even with the electric fans going day and night. At times we slept wrapped in wet sheets.

All that summer of 1927 I drove Mr. Wright daily to the office to work. One morning as I stopped and let him out, he came around and stood at the door to kiss me good-bye when the rear of a small truck pushed against his back. It turned out that the truck's reverse gear was stuck and it kept moving and pressing against him, pinning him to the car where I sat screaming helplessly. At first very pale, his face was getting red, his body pressed against our car. Several people ran to our help and pushed the truck which finally, roaringly, sped away. Mr. Wright stood, on his feet still, breathing heavily, but smiling proudly and pointing to the deep dent he had made in our car with the pressure of his body!

I burst into tears from mixed fright and joy that he was not injured. He had appeared to me as superhuman while he was being crushed between the truck

93

and the car. He said he had pressed his body with all his strength against the back of the truck. "This is an instance where man won over the machine," he said.

Providence seems to protect the fearless ones. He did not know fear. He had the strength of a man who meets life without wavering, indecision or doubt. Since he was given by Providence a courage unmatched, Providence must in turn protect him. There was an unwritten pledge between the two.

Once during the time when we used to drive with our Fellowship back and forth in caravan between Arizona and Wisconsin, we went off the beaten track, taking the way straight across the desert on what could barely be called an indication of a road which was supposed to lead us to Tuweep, a most beautiful part of that region, the northern side of the Grand Canyon. In the Indian language Tuweep means "good earth."

Ten miles after the turn-off we saw five horses and a post office and in the post office the postmaster warned us that Tuweep was seventy-five miles away with no gas station or any dwelling in between. The spirit of adventure was strong in us and our young people. We went ahead over the rockiest ground we had ever traveled on. Some tires went flat, some radiators boiled and so did some people's spirits. After we had traveled forty miles, stopping in the middle of no-where in the vast, rocky, barren desert, one of our young women, Betty Barnsdall, ran stumbling over the rocks toward our car and opened the door, screaming, "I cannot stand this any longer. I am tired. I don't want to go on!" she cried.

"Look, Betty," I said, "you are strong and young and healthy. If Mr. Wright and I can take it, you can."

She went back to the car crying and we went on. It was getting dark and when we reached what we thought was finally Tuweep it was already night. We unrolled our sleeping bags. Then, shivering in the cold of the night, we built a large fire. All were rather quiet, busily investigating their water levels in the radiators, and their gas levels in the tanks. Our supper was almost silent, but for Mr. Wright who felt fit, in good humor, his eyes bright as the fire burning before us. He said, "This is the only way to see our country."

People looked at him sadly because they hadn't seen anything for the last two hours. "This is the only way to travel," he went on. "One must go through hardships to enjoy leisure. People are getting too soft from too much soft living."

Betty was sniffling, blowing her nose. Others sat in admiration of him, while remembering the hard life of the winter in the cold desert tents we had just left behind. But everyone was silent.

"Yes," Mr. Wright continued, exhilarated, "this is what will make men and women out of you. Take a deep breath." He himself took one. "Enjoy this pure air. A human foot has probably not stepped on this ground for years. Just animals, snakes and birds. By the way," he added casually, "someone must keep the fire burning all night because we are in the country of mountain lions."

Young people's faces looked dark and pale with the shadows of flickering fire. Someone whispered to another, "Did you bring a gun along?"

95

"Thank God," the other said, "I did."

A young Polish woman, Marya Lilien, was there. She decided to cheer everybody up and volunteered to sing Russian songs.

"Goodness," someone whispered, "she has such a strong voice. What if we miss the mountain lion's snarl?"

But she bravely kept on her song for about an hour. She had a pleasant voice. Mr. Wright and I enjoyed her singing.

"Off to bed now!" he commanded. "We will all feel better in the morning."

People looked at him with doubt but started preparations for the night's sleep.

As soon as the sun came up, I opened my eyes to see Mr. Wright dressing with a deliberate slow tempo. I saw my breath as smoke. The snow was on the mountain range. He himself looked hewn out of granite, his strength as that of mountains.

Everyone else dressed shivering inside their sleeping bags. When we were ready we joined Mr. Wright standing at the edge of the Canyon just a few feet away from where he and I had unrolled our sleeping bags. . . . We didn't know that we had been so close to the precipice. Providence does take care of those whom it has blessed with courage.

As the sun rose, the Grand Canyon emerged out of the slow change of colors as a mirage created by the illusion of our vision. Forms appeared of delicate blues and lavenders, rose and greens—an unforgettable creation of nature. And it was as he said—everyone was full of spirit and vigor and ashamed of the doubts and fears of the night before.

We went back over the rocky trail drinking the beauty of what we saw in the early hours of the morning.

In the closing of the year 1958 Christmas boxes and bags were being rushed through our desert camp. Secret sessions were held by small groups. The "gift syndicates" were organized. No one was walking; everyone seemed to be in a terrible hurry.

Mr. Wright and I and many of our members were strictly forbidden to go near the part of the camp where our workshop is situated. At times I caught a glimpse of stained glass sticking out of some bags being taken into the shop. Cans of paint, nails, varnish, shellac, plastic and metals were swiftly carried through and if I carelessly asked the young people, "What in the world is going on here?" they smiled mysteriously and lied boldly, "Nothing, nothing at all."

"Is that so?" I remarked indifferently, also pretending that I was not the least bit interested.

Even the Taliesin children became secretive, vanishing through a narrow opening in the wall and back into the shop.

There was always one subject in our life together that really required a wise and delicate approach—the Christmas tree. Mr. Wright inevitably said every year, "It is ridiculous to have a Christmas tree in the desert. Why don't you hang your Christmas decoration on the ironwood tree in the patio?"

"But it is not the same. It is lovely to have a gay Christmas tree in the house."

"You are ruining this room," he would say irksomely. "You are destroying the lines by cluttering up the view."

"Goodness, there are three other sides of the room to which you can look and have views for miles—all the way from Superstition Mountain, circling Mc-Dowell Range up to Camelback Mountain. You only lose this tiny section of view. Can't you spare it for two weeks?"

"You don't get the idea," he would insist, looking down at me. "A Christmas tree does not belong in the desert."

"But I'm not importing it. There are fir trees growing just a few miles away from here. They naturally and organically grow on the mountainside."

"A few miles away! You mean eighty miles away!"

"Oh, that's nothing nowadays. Space has shrunk—remember?"

We always managed to get the tree in, but this was our classic dialogue every year and I was never certain that I might not lose next time.

Our boys usually drive to the mountains to get the tree just two days before Christmas. It is an adventure to which they always look forward. Besides the big tree, they bring several smaller ones for our apprentices with families.

The commercialism, the rush, the disappointments and frustrations of approaching Christmas, do not really touch the memory of true reverence to a great Man. Be it in the city stores with the continuous music of familiar carols or in the crowded streets where, above the horns of automobiles, one still hears the ringing of the bells and the chimes of the cathedrals. The idea of intensified giving and serving others in whatever form we can is there for us to take. Walking, waiting, leaning heavily on the counters, we see the tired faces of those who sell and those who buy, and this somehow binds us all together.

Here in the desert where the sky is close and the stars hang low, one's eyes search for the one that shone above the sacred premises where the new hope of the world was born. It happened in a country much like this desert where space is vast, the trees and shrubs sparse and airy, the mountains transparent—delicately drawn by the Master hand. One feels the presence of greatness without effort. In such solitude of vastness it is also easier to feel sorrow at the loss of those we have loved. . . .

But remembrance of immortality is strongly present, sealed by the birth of a Man who transformed revenge into love. Instead of an eye for an eye, a tooth for a tooth, the immortal words ring within us: "Love thine enemies."

What a great flight for human evolution! Even if we have made little progress, our wings tired and bruised during the ascent, through that great concept we have entered into a new spiritual era.

That is why I understand the tired faces of people in the stores and streets of the cities, have love for them that suffer because they cannot give as much as they wish, and share the sadness of many who can send only prayers to the loved ones they have lost.

Before dinner on Christmas Eve Mr. Wright and I sat together quietly in my room and I read aloud to him the Sermon on the Mount. I often stopped that we might contemplate the immortal words that no man can supersede. . . .

". . . Blessed are they which do hunger and thirst after righteousness: for they shall be filled. . . ."

". . . Blessed are the pure in heart: for they shall see God. . . ."

". . . For I say unto you, That except your righteousness shall exceed the righteousness of the scribes and Pharisees, ye shall in no case enter into the kingdom of heaven."

After dinner we went into the living room where the Christmas tree stood fragile, slim, this time decorated delicately with tiny flickering lights. We opened our presents by the large fireplace which blazed off and on as we threw in the wrappings.

Mr. Wright received many beautiful books on art, works of art, antique bowls, sculpture, wood carvings, handwoven shawls, stoles, robes. The members of our family exchanged gifts—my big brother, Vlado, and his wife, Sophie, glowed with pleasure, trying on clothes, smelling their perfumes and colognes. There were screams of delight from our daughter, Iovanna, and grandson, Brandoch. Towering Wes, Gene and our faithful engineer, Mendel Glickman, supported the occasion.

On the morning of the 25th, the Taliesin "gift syndicate" brought beautiful gifts to Mr. Wright and me.

100

John Rattenbury made two large glass mosaic tables for us of such extraordinary beauty that it was hard to take our eyes from them. Gene Masselink made a screen of unmatched beauty for our living room. It is of light cypress, and the design is carved, and cut through, with stained glass inserts and gold leaf. Mr. Wright stood the screen in just the right place in the Garden Room.

Several apprentices made an unusual wind-break of white plastic and plywood in a circular pattern for Mr. Wright's sun terrace. Many other beautiful works of art were made and given to us by our young people.

To various groups in the living room Mr. Wright and I distributed gifts. He spoke to them of the joy of giving and receiving. Before they left, Mr. Wright asked them to read the Sermon on the Mount.

Young faces were beautiful and receptive; those very new ones whom we knew for as short a time as a month appeared to come closer, cutting shorter the time it takes to become enlightened members of Taliesin.

Our lovely girls came in to receive gifts from us—they looked happy, radiant, with sunlight in their eyes —and those came who have been at Taliesin many years, those who have woven their lives with ours for twenty-five years or more.

From early morning and all day long, people forgot about themselves, giving to others gifts they had made or could afford to buy. Across the apprentice court, up the path to the Sun Cottage, down the bougainvillaea pergola, along the trails to the tents, caught on stag-horns and cholla of the desert the multicolored tin foils and gay ribbons sparkled in the sun. The Taliesin children ran back and forth happily, bright and excited with their gifts.

And when the evening came, we all gathered in the living room for the singing of the carols. The only guests that joined us on this Christmas occasion were Senator William Benton, his beautiful wife, and two of their children, Louise and John. John and Brandoch have been friends since childhood. They met shortly after the death of Brandoch's mother and have remained close through the years.

We stood up, some one hundred of us, and sang carols as we have done all the previous years. We particularly enjoyed singing "Silent Night." The voices were as one. When we walked to the theater the moon was already high, streaming down its pearly light and there was a feeling of union among us—a deep sense that only from the spirit issues the possession of life.

In the last week of 1958 every time Mr. Wright entered my room he said, "This is an awful room. It is all cluttered up. It has no sense of space. I don't see how you can live in it. Let me fix it up for you."

"But don't judge my room now," I objected. "A few days ago it was all cluttered up with the wrappings of Christmas packages to send and now I am still taking care of those that I received and I am writing 'thank you' letters. It just can't be helped."

"I know all that," he said, "but your furniture is ill-placed. Now, if I move your bed into this corner, throw that round table out, dispose of your two chairs, take those two lamps out . . ."

"You don't have to go further," I stated flatly. "I won't have it."

Raising both hands he said in an unusually quiescent way, "All right, live in this mess if you wish. People pay me thousands of dollars to do what I want to do for you."

It was that quiet way of his that touched me and worked in me during the following days. On New Year's Eve my conscience got the better of me and I said recklessly and tenderly, "You can fix my room and move the furniture as you want to." He gave me that wonderful swift look and there was an extremely brilliant sheen in his eyes.

On New Year's Day morning I got up early, ready for the change.

"Call in a couple of boys," he said. A little later the couple of boys called in another couple of boys and those called in more until my room was filled with eighteen people carrying out every solitary item!

The lights were torn out—which was necessary; the closet was torn out—also necessary; a gash in the rough stone wall was made and all the doors were taken off! I moved into the open Swan Cove, hearing Mr. Wright give architectural sermons on stone, glass and wood.

My room became a pile of rocks, lumber and sawdust; our New Year's Day became the most intense work day we had had since we arrived in the desert. Some of the young people who were not involved in it were jealous and envious and some were even hurt that they did not participate in the swirling delight of rush and turmoil. Of course it had to be a very cold day, as always happens on occasions of this kind, and the girls and I shivered, carrying my books, clothes, lamps, out into safety.

At the zenith of the fever, fervor and fury of action, a self-assured woman from a Columbus, Ohio, television station insisted on meeting Mr. Wright and me. We thought we were rather impatient with her but this did not affect her in the least. She roamed around freely, admiring and examining various objects, and suddenly made the astounding request that we either give her or sell her something from the room! I was stunned, but being very tired, I picked up the first thing I saw—a glass vase—and said, "Here, take it."

She protested that she could not carry it with her on the plane—would I please give her something more delicate, easier to handle? Mr. Wright, also wanting to free himself from this persistence, picked up some pretty star-encrusted paper napkins lying on the table and said, "Take these, you can put them in your purse."

"Good," she said. "I'll show them on TV and tell my audience what kind of beautiful work you do here."

"Oh, no," I exclaimed anxiously, quickly pulling the napkins out of Mr. Wright's and her hands. "Carol Robinson sent them to us for a Christmas present. We did not make them."

But she was not a bit discouraged. "Such nice lovely people like you," she fluttered, "are sure to find something that I can show my audience."

Mr. Wright and I exchanged bewildered looks and, momentarily forgetting her presence, I said loudly, "Why don't you give her the vase Aubrey made for you this Christmas? He will make you another."

"Good," she exclaimed uninhibitedly. "I'll take the

104

The Taliesin Fellowship at work:

Top—The Flower Triangle at Taliesin.

Center—One of the celebrated performances of Gilbert and Sullivan's "Patience," in the Pavilion at Taliesin West.

Bottom—A scene from the annual Festival of Music and Dance in the Pavilion; choreography and direction by Iovanna Lloyd Wright, music composed by Olgivanna Lloyd Wright, arranged by Bruce Brooks Pfeiffer and conducted by John Amarantides.

Mr. and Mrs. Wright at tea with some members of the
Fellowship, outside the drafting room at Taliesin West.

Frank Lloyd Wright at work with William Wesley Peters,
left, and Eugene Masselink, in the studio at Taliesin.

vase. Thanks a lot—nice to have met you. And I know I will see you again," and with a self-possessed stride she walked out of the room with the vase under her arm, headed for television.

Sometimes it is better not to attempt to classify human beings. Everyone is unique. I take it back that "the common man" exists—he is a myth—everyone is completely and absolutely uncommon!

When we went back to my wrecked room, Mr. Wright took out some of his resentment against the brashness of our visitor on me. I expressed, I thought quite modestly, a desire to have the new opening reach all the way to the floor. I was told coldly, with the perfect diction that only Mr. Wright possessed, that he could get along well without me. That he had had enough as it was.

I did not go to my room the rest of the day. Toward five o'clock in the afternoon, adjusting myself to my new quarters in the open Swan Cove, I shivered my way in and out of the icy wind. And when one apprentice came to see me after I had already discussed her problem the night before, I told her coldly, clearly and distinctly that she could get along well without me and that I had had enough as it was.

Even Madame Po, our little Chinese mother, looked grim when I saw her walking against the wind, and instead of the usual three bows, she gave me only one.

We all met in the theater for dinner and a movie. And now there was a transformation at Taliesin. The big work of the day was done; we told stories and laughed and we all agreed that it was the best New

107

Year's Day we had ever had. Our last New Year's Day with him.

Two weeks later Mr. Wright came to my room, which still smelled of paint and turpentine. "I can come in now without the feeling of oppression," he said. "Your room has a sense of space, simplicity and repose."

"I am so grateful to you for having done this for me," I answered.

The ceiling of my room is made of parallel redwood beams and boards under which runs a narrow band of square openings like a frieze with covered lights below them to make a pattern emphasizing the surface of the ceiling. The walls batter out and are painted a soft coral. The new window opens into a small garden. Beyond it extends the desert, covered with staghorns, saguaro and palo verde trees, to the far silhouettes of Black and Red Mountain, and farther away as though floating in the atmosphere is the delicately painted Superstition Range.

The glass doors on the other side run all the way up to the ceiling and I can look into my garden of green grass, sweet alyssum, pansies, blood-red bougainvillaea and the ironwood tree, so my room becomes part of the main garden. Two bronze deer appear to walk on the grass toward the terrace. And over the low grey stone wall, Camelback Mountain constantly changes its color.

My room is an office, a reception room, a study, a sewing room, a bedroom and a library. I have two desks now; one is for my secretary. The other I use for writing, reading, cutting materials, and designing. I have a

TV set. In case I become passive and tired, I can always turn it on to be infuriated by advertisers who treat us like retarded ten-year-olds. One can get plenty of energy from fury of this sort—supply enough to last for the whole day's work. But then, of course, television is at times a really wonderful medium which conveys events and the news of the world in a clear way, or presents great plays and comedies, however rare they may be.

Our valley is called Paradise Valley and it is truly beautiful. Years ago when Svetlana and Iovanna were small, we would drive out with them into the desert, through staghorn cactus, prickly pear, saguaros, the ocotillo with its red feather-like clusters of blossoms, and the dazzling, wicked cholla. We often stopped to crush the leaves of the grease-bush and inhaled its sharp medicinal odor, and we also crushed the silver-grey mock sage leaves that smelled deliciously like the pure mountain air. In the spring the desert floor was covered with tiny orange-colored blossoms and silver grass disappeared into the golden sands. Mr. Wright, the children and I were delighted when we came across the tumbleweeds rolling along leisurely and lightly on the desert roads. We sometimes stopped the car to watch a gila monster with orange beaded skin crawl slowly and clumsily in the dust.

In the later years of our life we still stopped, as we did then, to enjoy this vanishing desert life. And vanishing it is. A large part of the desert has been turned into fields of wheat and alfalfa. The ranches are becoming farms, with pasture land for cattle. The roads are being paved. Fences are springing up dividing small plots of real estate enterprises.

We were pioneers here twenty-five years ago, with the nearest residence twelve miles away. And now the valley is sprayed with houses and the lights at night are growing in number every year. Although it looks very pretty lighted like a carnival and although it is good to know that this dry land is being made fertile— we suffer the loss that goes with it—the wild life has almost left the Valley.

Deer still come occasionally to drink at the little fountains in the desert. But the coyotes with their weird howls have been practically exterminated. We used to hear their plaintive calls at night and at dawn. Man has continued to poison them to protect the sheep from their attacks. Maybe this mass poisoning has some justi-fication. I do not know.

Our friend Mrs. Philip K. Wrigley, who has a large house on a high hill opposite the Arizona Biltmore Hotel, told me one day in her gentle clear voice, "When we were married forty years ago Phil had a purebred Arabian stallion which he gave to me, and bought another for himself. Soon we purchased a mare and began raising Arabians at our ranch on Catalina Island, a few miles off the coast of Southern California. Now our herd has increased to 150 purebred Arabians."

When Mr. and Mrs. Wrigley and Mr. and Mrs. Fowler McCormick renewed their acquaintance in Arizona they inspired each other to sponsor the Arabian horse shows. Philip Wrigley owns the Biltmore Hotel and they first gave a little exhibit together at the Biltmore Stables. In the last six years it has developed into the largest Arabian horse show in the country. One year the entries surpassed even those of the Cow Palace show in San Francisco which is reputed to be the largest of all. The Arabian show was held at the Mc-Cormick Ranch just below Taliesin West and when Mrs. Wrigley invited us to be their guests we were happy to accept.

That Saturday afternoon proved to be the most tempestuous since we arrived in Arizona. Mr. Wright and I were driving down the Taliesin Road when we met our grandson, Brandoch, who ran up to us saying breathlessly, "Don't go down—everyone is leaving the show—you can't see a thing. The dust storm is terrible." But we were determined to go.

Our camp is elevated from the desert floor and protected by the mountains. On the level ground strong Desert Devils—the wind blasts—struck the windows of our car with a shower of dust and pebbles. The further down we drove into the plains the stronger the wind became. The blasts of dust were now continuous. By the time we reached the last mile of the road leading to the horse show we met endless lines of returning cars slowly crawling, with lights on, glowing pale, barely visible, a few feet away. But neither Mr. Wright nor I wanted to turn back.

Driving into the grounds we saw people frantically running, scarves covering their noses and mouths, almost pushed by the wind into their cars. The sheriff and his deputies were uselessly waving their arms shouting, "No!" "Stop!" "Turn right!" "Turn left!" "Go back!"—but we, of course, drove right ahead. We passed the picturesque riders magnificently dressed in genuine Arabian attire. Their cloaks and the tails of the horses flew with the violence of the wind. The headdresses of some of the women riders had been blown off and their hair waved wildly, covered with dust.

Dick Carney drove us right onto the track all the way to the boxes which were empty but for a few horse devotees who sat shivering and occasionally covering their noses and mouths when the wind spasmodically struck the hanging clouds of dust.

No normal person, I am certain, would have stayed through the dust-anguish except the horse addict! Philip and Helen Wrigley were nowhere in sight—the storm had driven them out. However, the show went on just the same. We were most fortunate to be able to watch from our tightly closed car. It was a superb sight. The fantastic, gorgeous Arabian creatures stepped with grace, arching their strong necks, and looking with disdain on their human contemporaries. Snobbish, aristocratic, their heads raised high, they kept walking, trotting, cantering in the ring while their riders' flowing robes whipped at their flanks. The desert, the dust and the wind were in tune with the dashing Arabians.

When Brandoch was six he often had breakfast with Mr. Wright and me. On the wall above our table hung an Indian painting of a galloping pink horse. Our breakfast was at seven o'clock and Brandoch was frequently late. Mr. Wright said one morning, "You see that pink horse? Whoever arrives first in the morning will ride him." Next morning Brandoch rushed to the cove to find Mr. Wright already there. He burst into tears.

At breakfast the following day Brandoch was sitting at the table with a happy face. "I am riding the pink horse today," he exclaimed. The painting came alive for all three of us; it started our day at a swift pace.

Brandoch today is an early riser. He gets up at five in the morning to practice on his 'cello and likes it. I attribute his good habit to our morning rides on the pink horse.

One morning I invited the Taliesin children to my room for a party. It was a lovely beginning! We ate cookies and cakes, we drank 7-Up, nibbled candies and looked at television—each one loudly guessing which way the story would end and finally we settled into a "conversation."

"What do you like to do best?" I asked.

"I like to sleep outside of my tent under the moon," said Leslie, who was ten.

"And I like to visit Shawn and talk with her for a long, long time before we go to sleep," her friend Celeste confessed.

"And I prefer to read," said twelve-year-old Brian with snobbish superiority.

And then somehow there started a turmoil—everyone shouted at once.

"I like to swing."

"I like to study about Presidents of the United States. You want me to tell them to you? I know ten Presidents!" Ronnie bragged at eleven.

"Wait," I said, "not just now!"

". . . I like best to swing in a swing. I wish I could swing all my life! Let us get more swings!"

"I want to go to Siam and see the temples. Let's all go to Siam! Will you take us to Siam?" little Shawn Rorke said dreamily.

"Maybe. Stop your noise, will you?"

"May I tell you now about the Presidents?"

"I want to be a 'rock hound'."

"I want to go to Japan—let's go to Japan."

"Susy stepped on my foot!" Margie howled.

"Stop your crying," I said. "It cannot hurt that much —Susy is not an elephant."

They thought this very funny. And while Margie screamed they began to revel in such torrents of laughter that there was no stopping them. . . .

In the meantime my dog, Casanova, with a wild look in his eyes was yelping and squeezing in through the children, trying to get to me. At the pitch of this uninhibited abandon, Allen Davison came in with a camera and asked quietly, "May I take a picture of all of you?" And suddenly, from pinching, whirling, hitting, screaming, pushing, the children turned into angelic creatures and with the sweetest expression on their faces they looked up at the bougainvillaea blossoms streaming in red streaks from the roof of my garden. . . .

Our last Easter preparations with Mr. Wright in our life began on Good Friday. Some of our young people went to church, many read the Bible, and all joined together later to help with the work.

My room was littered with our cookbooks and recipes of former years. We enjoyed going over our archaic

114

description of the making of Baba, the tall Russian Easter bread. Each recipe is marked by the year it was used and each year it is modified and improved. All the faults of the last year have been duly recorded and the changes added to the method of work itself. This archaic and complicated recipe that only we can understand was used in 1959:

Saturday. 6:00 a.m. Light the large and small ovens at 250°. Four people start separating the eggs. Put the large new can by stove with rocks in the bottom to weigh it down and place bread bowls on top of can. Mix Baba batter and put to rise.

7:00 a.m. Assign two boys to make, of thick paper, twenty-five circular forms, eleven inches high and seven inches in diameter. Line with wax paper.

8:00 a.m. Get Kleenex in case we need it to wipe perspiration, two bowls of water, eight table-knives to scrape hands, soap and clean towels. Ask twenty boys and six girls to wash their hands. Two will hold bread pan; one will pour eggs; one adds lemons, vanilla, salt and butter. (Lunch will have to be cooked in the little kitchen.)

9:20 a.m. Dough is ready when double in bulk. Move bread pan gently from griddle to large can and add rest of ingredients.

9:30 a.m. Call the boys, have them again wash their hands thoroughly. Clip their fingernails, and form two lines on each side of the bread pan. Two must always hold the pan. (To remove any possible kerosene or gasoline odor from hands, clean with vinegar and salt.) Twenty boys beat Baba, four at a time, and two hold pan. Don't be too gay at first. You may regret it! When the dough is very sticky and thin, butter hands slightly, after beating. Six girls scrape dough off with a table knife. Be careful not to lose a particle of dough—it is like losing a slice of Baba. The next person in line takes the dough from the one just having beaten. Change beaters every ten seconds. Do not stop beating, no matter what! Then later, when the dough hardly sticks, wash hands again and dry thoroughly—it will stick less and make beating easier. Do not use butter on hands after the first twenty minutes. Do not worry that the dough looks thin. Do not stop after the first bubble; do not stop beating for one hour and ten minutes! Someone wipe perspiration off foreheads! Someone have pencil to write down any change in recipe. Someone record time. Do not scrape off the sides anymore when the large bubbles show. Keep containers warm. Divide the dough into four parts and put into warm containers. Put back on stove to rise. Cover with cotton flannel sheets and one wool blanket. Check to see that it does not get too hot or too cold.

11:30 a.m. Put the paper forms on the table; butter them inside very carefully so as to not leave one spot unbuttered for it will tear the Baba.

1:15 p.m. Baba has tripled in size. Put one of the containers on the dining table. One person stands by counter, hands Mrs. Wright a form to fill one-third full, another stands by the stove, to immediately put the filled form back in a warm place—on top of one-inch thick board on the stove. Cover with cotton flannel sheet and wool blanket again and let rise until three-quarters full.

Approximate time of baking: one hour and fifteen minutes in oven. Clean dining tables, get eighteen pillows and cover with dish-towels. Get scissors and towels to hold and open Baba forms with. Do not look in ovens! You may interfere with the rising of the Babas. Only Mrs. Wright should do this. If the paper smokes, do not worry! It should. Take Babas out; carefully tip them onto a pillow, gently pulling off the form. If this does not work, rip or cut form off; carefully tear off wax paper, starting on the darker side, toward the light. If it pulls the Baba off, stop pulling! Gently roll Baba on pillow, turning occasionally until it is quite firm. Take to dining room; put on tables, still turning occasionally. Check that the children and the dogs cannot get to Babas, and then—relax!

This is quoted directly from the authentic documentary recipe compiled from previous years of accumulated experience.

People were running in and out of my room. We held consultations pertaining to table arrangements, seating of guests and apprentices, timing of ensemble and chorus music and the general plan for Saturday and Sunday. John Amarantides, the director of music, was working on programs, Eugene Masselink was again booking the film, *The Day of Triumph*, which we have shown every Easter morning. It is like reading the Bible. We see and hear the story of Jesus, who 2000 years ago proclaimed that love is the way to immortality. He died for His faith. We need His inspiration—

117

we need every reminder, even the food, to commemorate Him.

Although Easter has been defined by some historians as a continuation of the pagan Spring Festival, in no way does that exclude the idea that the resurrection of Christ simply coincided with it. Thus the egg for the pagan was a symbol of fertility; with the Resurrection it became the symbol of continuity, of eternity.

In ancient times the egg was dyed only red, representing eternity sealed and proved by the blood of Christ. The bread was always considered the staff of life. The Russians made the bread festive, the ingredients rich, and as tall as their ovens would bake it. On the top of Baba it is customary to stamp the cross made of icing. And the white pascha—symbol of purity—is made out of cheese, eggs, cream, butter and almonds. Its shape is pyramidal, each side being marked with the cross. Thus all food for the Easter celebration from ancient times until now is blessed by memory and promise of life eternal.

At Taliesin West, our cathedral is the desert and its dome the sky.

Easter Day on April first was the happiest one of all the thirty-seven years of our life together. It was a beautiful morning, full of sunlight. We both dressed in white. I went early to Mr. Wright's room to wish him a Happy Easter. We walked out to greet our young people and our guests.

Balloons flew everywhere. Tables were spread with

flowers, Babas rose from circles of multicolored eggs, the pascha cheese shimmered white in garlands of blossoms and leaves. We sat down at the long row of tables and listened to the singing of our choir—the voices rose, the music echoed in the vastness of the desert space and sky. We ate gaily and like children broke the eggs end to end. Happy and free we laughed, immersed in purity of spirit.

Mr. Wright and I then walked arm in arm to our theater, followed by our friends and young people. We saw again *The Day of Triumph;* and this beautiful film once more turned back the pages of history for us. Arm in arm we walked back to our rooms to talk, to meditate, to rest, to be in each other's presence.

The day kept the sun, and the early evening sky was painted red. We walked together to the pavilion to listen to our friend Carol Robinson play Beethoven. Mr. Wright spoke of Beethoven, calling him "an architect of music, great master, the greatest of them all."

We listened to the music for a long time. Four of his children were there—Lloyd and his wife, Helen; David and his wife, Gladys; Catherine and her husband, Kenneth Baxter; Iovanna of course; his granddaughter, Anne; his grandson, Eric—the last Easter with their father and grandfather.

At the end of the evening, he and I arm in arm walked happily back to our rooms. It was our last Easter together.

On April ninth came the end of a great life.

Following her visit to Taliesin West on the weekend of April 26, 1959, Margaret Sanger, the famous crusader for Planned Parenthood, wrote to me:

". . . You are in my thoughts day after day. It was so good of you to let me come for the night last Saturday and to be at your wonderful Sunday breakfast.

"Your courage and determination to keep things going as Frank had them is a most inspiring, uplifting help to all your friends. So few left behind can *know* what to do, but in your living with Frank as *one* together, you grew to adulthood under his wing. He *too* grew in spiritual values, as shown in his later designs, by being with you and loving you.

"I realize that in death like birth one must go it alone. Nothing one can say to you can fill the loneliness of your heart. But do, please, believe me when I say: your head up, your following in Frank's ways, does much for your friends and for their faith in God.

"I went to you dreading to feel the gap in the Taliesin atmosphere. There was *none*. It was alive, as only you could give it life. A thousand blessings come from Frank's spirit—that I know. He is near you hourly; he is too great a spirit to leave you. He lives on and on beside you. . . ."

At breakfast the next Sunday I spoke to the Fellowship about our life and work after reading the following paragraphs from one of Mr. Wright's addresses to our apprentices:

". . . What would have happened if we'd had an architect coming over on the Mayflower who was familiar with the organic principles that motivate us here at Taliesin? We would have a great culture now, instead of none, and inasmuch as architecture is the cornerstone of any true culture whatsoever, you are much the most important members of this body politic we call the United States of America. And you are the most needed. And you have before you one of the greatest careers, in all probability.

"If you can learn to *see in* and learn to build as you ought to learn to build, you will be the great saviours, probably, of your civilization in your day. Because more than to any other member of society comes the opportunity to you to shape, to determine the shape of things to come. You are shape-hewers and shape-knowers or you are not architects at heart. And, of course, it takes a long time to make that kind of an architect. You cannot jump into it. You cannot get it by wishing to be it. Unfortunately, too, you cannot be it by just thinking you are it.

". . . We don't want you all to be alike, we don't want you all to think alike; but we do want you all to know the basis of the thought that makes an architect at heart."

I then spoke: "Mr. Wright always claimed that any one of our boys who worked productively with us for some years would do as well or better than any practicing architect in the world today. There was strength in that conviction. I understand it because you have been trained to study structure from every point of view. And those of you who have been developed as complete individuals will naturally create the exterior forms of architecture from within.

"The plan of Taliesin life from the beginning has

been to contribute to the development of the individual. Both Mr. Wright and I valued individuality most of all. In order to achieve it you must rid yourself of opinionatedness which you may frequently mistake for your convictions. You could not possibly generate ideas as an individual if you allow your opinionatedness to interfere with your receptivity. You have to discard it in order to make room to give your mind a chance to work creatively.

"If we placed you immediately at the drafting board and you did nothing but drafting all day, your brain would start to form ruts; but with the changes of work that we give you at Taliesin that cannot happen.

"I do not believe anyone who has been here several years could possibly fall into any superficial limitations —he would want to touch depth. Paul Tillich, Doctor of Theology at the Harvard Divinity School, was speaking of the lack of this very thing in our civilization— he called it 'depth dimension.' By the way, he is an interesting man to meet; he has depth himself and speaks eloquently. He sent me a book entitled *The Courage to Be*. The title was exciting, but the book was full of quotations and I was sorry to lose him among the quotations.

"If you want to develop individuality, you should be able to work harmoniously with all kinds of people. The more people you accept with tolerance of their shortcomings, the more understanding you gain. The fewer you accept, the tighter you will become, the more introverted; consequently the less developed and the less creative.

"Unfortunately much too often artistically inclined

122

people are introverts by nature. If you are only an introvert, the world will be passing by you and you will be looking at it from way down somewhere, having no part in it.

"The thorough extrovert is an airy personality, often lacking the 'depth dimension,' whereas the thorough introvert is sometimes unable to see the sunlit spaces of inspiration.

"Only when introvert and extrovert qualities are in proper measure are you a fully developed and contributing member of society. It is your choice to experience a whole scale of human expression in all forms, in all ways.

"It takes daily contact in work together to know one another—to know who has ability to carry his work through; who has a sense of responsibility and the strength to be."

Chapter 5

TALIESIN NORTH—WISCONSIN

The preparations for June Eighth, the Memorial Dinner, reached every corner of Taliesin and Hillside.

After we returned from the desert, projects from all directions avalanched upon us. However, everyone welcomed the intense activity of our days. The broken wall of the upper dam had to be rebuilt in time; the pool in front of Mr. Wright's room repaired and repainted; the interior of the rooms re-arranged, the grounds cleared and mowed, the flowers planted all over Taliesin and Hillside including the triangle gardens on the highway.

And the little chapel in our valley had a new head stone added to its grounds . . .

The work in the drafting room had to go on uninterrupted. The drawings and models had to be sorted, packed and shipped for the exhibition at the Metropolitan Museum which opened June eighth.

Relatives and friends arrived from near and far. Three of Mr. Wright's four sons and their wives came from different parts of the country to honor their father. Mr. Wright was very proud of his children.

Lloyd Wright, the eldest son, a sensitive artist, a

visionary architect, came with his diminutive, stylish wife, Helen. Mr. Wright often praised his fine architectural work. He has built many buildings; the most famous among them, and the most written about, is the Wayfarer's Chapel. Many pilgrim-tourists stop at the little chapel on the Southern California coast to gain inspiration from its superb lines of wood entirely sheeted with glass, creating an ethereal, religious atmosphere.

John Lloyd Wright, the second son, who was not able to come, is a gifted architect who adheres to his father's architectural principles. His wife, Frances, is a talented artist and writer.

Mr. Wright's third son, David, is a successful manufacturer of building materials. With his handsome wife, Gladys, he has built a home in Phoenix, Arizona, designed by his father, which both of them love and cherish.

Robert Llewellyn Wright, the youngest son, a prominent lawyer in Washington, D. C., was present with his lovely wife, Betty, whose father Mr. Wright knew and admired. Llewellyn, too, had his father design and build a house for them in Bethesda, Maryland.

Mr. Wright's daughter, Catherine, who also was unable to attend is married to Kenneth Baxter, an accomplished businessman. Swift of mind and artistic, she does beautiful work as an interior decorator and fashioner of decorative objects. She is the mother of Anne Baxter, of stage and cinema.

The youngest daughter, the late Frances Caroe, was also a designer and artist who devoted many years of her life to America House in New York, promoting American crafts and arts.

Then there were Mr. Wright's sister, the artist, Maginel Wright Barney, with her daughter, Elizabeth Enright Gillham, the noted writer; grandchildren Anne Baxter, Eric Lloyd Wright, Nora Natof; nieces and nephews, among them Franklin Porter and his wife Mary, Jenkin Lloyd Jones, the editor of the *Tulsa Tribune*; and many grandnieces and grandnephews.

The sons reminisced about their past life: their hikes and walks among the Wisconsin green hills and meadows, gathering wild flowers. They smiled when I related to them the many times Mr. Wright spoke of a little incident that had imprinted itself unforgettably upon his heart. He and Lloyd were walking over the hill opposite Taliesin. The thirteen-year-old boy stopped, dropped down on his knees, stretching out his arms, and called out in his deep, husky voice, "Oh, Father! The flowers—they are violets!" Mr. Wright said the expression of the young lad's face was of such joy at the sight of the purple patch on the green that it brought tears to his eyes. And whenever he told the story, though laughing with pleasure, their father's eyes were misted with tears . . .

David reminisced about how he had earned twenty dollars one entire summer while working for his great Uncle James from six in the morning until six at night. He teased his brothers, "You fellows—you were only visitors!"

Llewellyn laughed. "Oh, no! I worked on the farm, but my wages were cut in half because I spilled a few gallons of milk!"

There was Grandson Eric, the son of Lloyd, who spent some years at Taliesin as an apprentice. He was a little curly-headed boy of seven when he asked me, "Is it true that you really are my grandmother?"

"Of course, I am," I answered. "I'm your grandmother in spirit." He appeared to be satisfied.

Years later when Eric was sixteen, while introducing him to some of my friends, I said, "This is my stepgrandson."

"Gee," Eric turned toward me, "I wish you'd skip that 'step'!"

And when Grandson Tommy, Llewellyn's son, was twelve years old, spending his summer at Taliesin, his grandfather and I took him to tea at Baron's Tea Room in Madison. Tommy was a very serious boy. He looked at me appraisingly and said gravely, "Grandmother, I approve of the hat you are wearing today."

Granddaughter Nora, the only child of the late Frances Wright Caroe, visited Taliesin also at the age of sixteen. John deKoven Hill, our apprentice, became quite worried when early each morning he would hear her voice below his room saying, "Johnny, stop it. Are you crazy? . . . Move over . . . That's all right, Johnny. I love you. You know that . . . Ouch! Don't do that! Stop it!"

John Hill discovered quite a bit later that it was Johnny Walker—Mr. Wright's horse—she was talking to!

And so went the reminiscences with our family, lightening the weight of unspoken thoughts, releasing for a time the strain of the pressing present.

The following are speeches delivered at the Memorial Dinner.

127

William T. Evjue, Editor and Publisher of the *Capital Times:*

"In the months of March of 1958 and 1959 I spent several weeks each year at Taliesin West as the guest of Mr. and Mrs. Wright. I rate these visits to Taliesin as among the greatest experiences of my life.

"We sat for an hour and a half at the breakfast table at times. At least three cups of coffee were poured while we discussed such subjects as the origin of the universe, the lack of culture in the United States, that war still remained as the only method by which mankind could settle its disputes, the failure of education, the continued surrender of government to an alliance of big business and the military, and much talk in which the word 'organic' was used.

"One morning at breakfast I asked Mr. Wright about the word 'organic' which he used so frequently. I said: 'Mr. Wright, do you remember when we were on the Nakoma golf course years ago after you had been invited to draw plans for a new Nakoma clubhouse? Do you remember that I had asked you then to give me your definition of the word organic?'

"Mr. Wright looked down the fairway on which we were standing, leaned over to pick up a handful of Nakoma soil which he patted flat in the palm of his hand, and said: 'That's what I mean when I use the word organic.'

"It was about the time he was contending that the United States should have a prairie architecture indigenous to its own soil and character, and that the use of the ancient forms of architecture in Italy, France and

128

England should not have priority in a great land like the United States.

"I asked Mr. Wright about his concept of God. I asked this question in the midst of the flaming bougainvillaea on the premises and the beautiful desert flowers which were beginning to appear. Mr. Wright said quickly:

" 'Nature is my manifestation of God. I go to Nature every day for inspiration in the day's work. I follow in building the principles which Nature has used in its domain.'

"Mrs. Wright's dog, Casanova, was there too, at the breakfast table but he stretched out in slumber as world problems were being solved at the breakfast table.

"Following Mr. Wright's death, the newspaper with which I am associated said:

" 'To Mr. Wright, nothing was more precious than freedom; nothing more hateful than the government or the social customs that bound the freedom of expressions and movements that he considered necessary to the development of human dignity. He fought his battles in the world of ideas; he never ducked a battle and never gave quarter. He despised the stupidity of war. It is in the world of ideas that his enduring monument will be found. His thought is part of the stream of human life and nothing but complete annihilation can remove it.

" 'There is nothing that can destroy an idea that has the power of truth and beauty. Frank Lloyd Wright gave the world some of those ideas, and he lived his life in the faith that only in leaving enduring ideas can man give the world a lasting heritage.'

"What a wonderful legacy has been left to Mrs. Wright and the members of the Taliesin Fellowship— the privilege and responsibility of carrying on the work of a great teacher.

"Mrs. Wright is well equipped to accept this responsibility. She was at his side for many years, vigilantly watching his health and steadfastly carrying out the countless and varied tasks that she assumed in the partnership she and Mr. Wright enjoyed.

"What a comfort it must be for her to know that she is surrounded by a group of dedicated young men and women, some of whom have been with Mr. Wright for twenty years and more and others for ten years and more.

"They know the goals that Mr. Wright set. They have been given the tools of his inspiration. They will work ahead to make this a more beautiful country in which to live . . ."

Harold C. Price, Sr.:

"Most of you here have known Mr. Wright far longer than I have. Miss Alicia Patterson asked me a few minutes ago how I happened to contact Mr. Wright to build the tower. The answer is this:

"In 1952, or about seven years ago, my two young sons suggested that I get hold of the best architect that could be found, a man who was always young—Mr. Wright. We came to Taliesin in that year, 1952, with one thing in mind—to build a three-story building for our own use, covering 25,000 square feet. Mr. Wright immediately and instantaneously vetoed that idea and suggested that we build a ten-story building covering the same amount of floor space. Ultimately we compromised, and built one nineteen stories high!

"Since then he has built two homes for our family—one in Oklahoma and one in Arizona.

"And there is only one more thing I want to say: That we of the company and we of the family think we are greatly priviliged and always will be to live in an edifice designed by Frank Lloyd Wright."

Alicia Patterson Guggenheim:

"I am proud to be here tonight and I think we are all so fortunate to be here tonight. We were fortunate to have been the friends of such a remarkable man as Frank Lloyd Wright. This fortune comes to few people. I wish I had known him longer. But I feel very proud that I knew him as long as I did. He was the uncommon man. The man who could build buildings that were flung across the whole world and will continue to stand as a monument to this greatness. And every building, whether it happened to have been a house for someone to live in, or a great building, such as he built for Mr. Price or the Museum in New York—were all dedicated so lovingly to Nature, which he loved. Because as Mr. Evjue said, 'To him Nature was everything. Nature was all the body of God that man would ever see,' as he used to say.

"But somehow it is not as a great architect that I remember him, it is as a great man who fought all of his long and useful life against sham and hypocrisy, who refused to bow to the great god, Organization. And who felt that the individual was more important than the mass.

"Because he did this he made some enemies. People said that he was egotistical, and people said that he was difficult, and people said that he was intolerant. He did not care a bit because he knew where he was going. But he had the courage and his path was hard—the one he took. So he created a Foundation to make the paths of those who believe in his ideas a little easier. And he put his beloved wife in charge—with Wesley Peters, his son-in-law, and Eugene Masselink. Those three and all the others beside them will follow, I am sure, and carry on his tradition. Because if they do, Frank Lloyd Wright will never die. And that high star that he hitched his wagon to will shine on."

Buckminster Fuller:

"Mr. Wright asked me to speak at Taliesin when I visited here several times. And when Mr. Wright asked me to speak, I felt very wonderful about it. It is quite extraordinary to stand up here now and think about it. It is quite extraordinary to stand up here now and think about speaking at Taliesin, and not have Mr. Wright say, 'Bucky, I'd like you to speak to my friends, my fellows.'

"Mrs. Wright will probably remember the first time that I ever met Mr. Wright and herself. In 1930 they were having a symposium on modern architecture in New York at the Women's University Club. Not everybody here will remember 1930, it is now getting to be some years ago. But it was the depth of the depression and there were some great buildings that had been undertaken and some wondered whether those buildings would ever be finished. The Empire State had been started and architects who were asked to speak on modern architecture to the Women's University were the men who were the designers of those great buildings. The Chrysler building was about to open its doors a few months later. Raymond Hood's News Building was his largest building. The Radio City had not been undertaken.

"The architect for the Empire State Building which was about to be built spoke. I couldn't understand how it happened that I had been invited to speak on this symposium because I had never built a building. I was a researcher. And I never knew just what it was all about until, having spoken and sat down, I found that I was simply the punctuation mark between these other speakers! Mr. Wright was to be the last speaker.

"And when I sat down, after having said something about research and building, Mr. Wright stood up and said, 'My young friend, Buckminster, is as bad a speaker as he is good as a designer.' And from that time on he befriended me. And of all the befriendings I have ever had, there is none that has given me such courage and pride.

"It is particularly interesting that he befriended me because my kind of work was in very stark, scientific lines. I loved what he did and, like all human beings, I had a very soft spot for the extraordinary beauty, tenderness and feeling that he had. In my work I was trying to put on blinders with regard to what things looked like. I was simply interested in structural prin-

133

ciples and this man kept on being my friend, saying 'I love you for just paying attention to your structural principles. That's what God gave you the capability to do and you seem to be able to keep on doing it.'

"No matter what I did, stark as it might be, Frank seemed to get warmer and warmer. Then came the first visit to Taliesin in 1938 and we had a wonderful meeting. I remember saying 'I didn't know that human beings could live in such a wonderful way as this.' It was certainly a new experience to me. I am a New Englander and was brought up in my very Puritan way. I was brought up with sort of the idea that you were constricted by the society and had a great deal to conform to. Frank Wright wasn't breaking through anything in any unfriendly way, but he just seemed to have the ability to establish something like heaven here. And here I was invited to come and visit 'heaven.' And then I was asked to speak at 'heaven' and the idea of my having anything to say there just seemed preposterous. Just as preposterous as tonight. The only reason that I am doing it is because I love him so and I look down at the end of the room and see on the wall that wonderful face, that great strength, that smile, that drive-through; and I said 'I am going to be very proud to stand up here.'

"In my stark way I am a student of patterns and I have tried to be a student of large patterns. And I think it is very difficult for most people to deal in the large patterns. Life seems to try to force us to look at the small ones.

"Frank Lloyd Wright was thirty-five years old when the airplane was invented; an age at which most young men would pretty well have formed the lines of the way they were going to think. Certainly this man brought through, more vigorously than any other I know, a real tradition of man on earth; man living up to what God gave him the capability for—dedication to love, beauty, and the daring to be intimate with Nature.

"This man carried forward an appreciation and understanding of tradition. I am quite sure that in big patterns, he represented the great closing of the round-the-world pattern that started millenniums ago, the pattern of western-bound man.

"When Frank Wright went to the Orient from America, he, I think, closed the gap of man-around-the-world. He brought into this cross-breeding, young, democratic America, on this continent, an awareness of the extraordinary tradition of the Orient, thousands and thousands of years old, and then had the ability to meet the age of the airplane and to go forward into this unprecedented acceleration of man around the earth; And in such a manner as not only to meet it and welcome it, but to give great strength and courage to all those explorers in the new kinds of invisible doings which are for the moment perplexing all men because they can't see the areas of our great explorations. Frank Wright really went all out for history yet affirmed: 'I have great faith in what is coming upon us!' There is no question about it. Frank Wright, as the ages go by, will be seen as the great architect who was responsible for carrying the Old forward into the New; and thereby really gave us what I, as a student of pattern, might not have been given otherwise. He kept the door open

135

for real appreciation of and dedication to the knowledge and the creative gifts of man throughout history."

Adlai Stevenson:
"Mr. Buckminster Fuller has just told us that as a young man he came from New England, that he never had expected he would be invited both to visit in heaven and to speak in heaven. Well, I come from the prairies of Illinois, and it is exactly the same with me, sir. Moreover, speaking in 'heaven' about 'heaven' in these circumstances also suggests the total futility of what I might have to add to what has already preceded me this evening . . . You all know, perhaps better than I, about Frank Lloyd Wright.

"It made me think of the unhappy tale of the American missionary who was trying, Mrs. Wright, to explain to a Confucian scholar the concept of the Holy Trinity. And after some time, after he had explained at length, the old Confucian said, 'But, sir, then you have not one but three Gods!' The missionary sighed and started all over again; explained again about the Father, the Son, and the Holy Ghost. And finally, with a great light spread across his face, the old Chinese turned to the missionary, 'Ah! What a typically American solution—a committee!'

"Well, we had a committee! The committee has reported and anything that I have to say is by way of fruitless postscript, I am afraid.

"I know all of you were deeply moved by the portrait of the beauty of this man that Olgivanna Wright has given us here this evening. She used phrases like

136

'the integrity of the individual,' 'truth held high.' These I suppose are more meaningful about him than anything I could possibly say.

"But her words were more, it seemed to me, than the words of partnership, of collaboration, of involvement, indeed of love. They were the anatomy of a great spirit as well as a great genius. And I, for one, should like to thank you, Mrs. Wright, not only for the evening that we have enjoyed here, but for the lovely tribute to a human being, to an American that we all admire, respect and love. Likewise I am impressed most deeply by what Bill Evjue of the Madison *Capital Times* had to say about the gallant, remorseless champion of truth —Mr. Frank Lloyd Wright: 'He never ducked a battle' I believe he said. And I could add to that, sir, that neither have you ever ducked a battle.

"The words of Mr. Price and those of Alicia Patterson, who spoke from the fullness of her heart, and also the words of Mr. Fuller, left me with nothing to add but this: Few people leave any impression on their generation, on their time. Even fewer leave indelible footprints on more than one or two generations—but this man did. Not alone because he was a great artist; not alone because he contributed something new to the store of human culture, to the understanding, the insights of the West; but also because he had ideas. What impressed me even more in my meetings with him over a period of years—at Lloyd Lewis's house in Chicago; in New York; and in Arizona—was his love of life.

"I must say to you that the best thing I ever got into was life. I'm so glad that I didn't miss it. And I have the feeling Mr. Wright felt that way about life—

he was glad to be in it; he knew it was for the living. There are those immortal words in the Twenty-seventh Psalm: 'I had fainted unless I had believed to see the goodness of the Lord in the Land of the Living.' Mr. Frank Lloyd Wright was very much in the land of the living. There he found the goodness because he brought goodness, because he created goodness, because he made beauty, because he built an immortal chapter into the continuity of western civilization. And for that I, like any citizen of our land, of our culture, will be everlastingly grateful.

"But I am sure that far more than our dinner, far more than the poor testimonials of living men that we can make here, he would be impressed not indeed by his immortal monuments in stone, not by these—his works that will live so long—but by the continuity of flesh and blood, by the continuity of this Fellowship, by the idea. There is something in the Scriptures about the Grace of Continuity. It is a wonderful phrase, the Grace of Continuity. Somehow to keep the continuity of this grove of academia, this Fellowship, this dedication, the purity of an aspect of the arts to their enlargement, their elevation, their grandeur, is the most generous tribute that we could pay him. And for that we have not only the members of the Fellowship to pay our homage to, but most of all, to Olgivanna Wright. Under her inspiration, with the help I am sure of all of you and of these who have come here to labor, by virtue not only of their love of Frank Lloyd Wright, but most of all of their love of art, this work will be continued. It will be continued for the greater glory

Monthly presentation of student projects and drawings—shown for criticism and guidance, in terms of organic architecture, by Mrs. Wright, William Wesley Peters, Eugene Masselink and John Howe (seated extreme right).

Some members of the Fellowship at work in the drafting room at Taliesin.

not of man alone, not of Frank Lloyd Wright alone, but of what we all esteem even higher, which is our civilization."

Yet how frequently men in our civilization can fail to see greatness before them, how confused their vision can become.

About *twenty-five years ago* one of our less endowed members, both mentally and architecturally, said foolishly but bluntly, "Mr. Wright is too old now to be a creative designer. He should retire so that we can take his place in architecture."

I was shocked at such blindness. Afterwards I thought that this may be the reaction of other people who still count a man's age in numerals.

In the years since, Mr. Wright's great creative force, the limit of which could not be seen, kept reaching higher and higher. He created in the abundance of his imaginative spirit still greater buildings that kept startling the world, shocking the engineers with his daring trespassings of established formulas, inspiring the young generation with ever new, exciting, architectural forms. Time was being dissolved by him as he moved up with every step of his life.

A well known architect of today was at one time a member of the Taliesin Fellowship. Many years ago he came to visit us in the desert. He had deep affection and appreciation for Mr. Wright and his work. Yet even he must have become suddenly lost in the maze of

141

dated, abandoned measures. Standing on the sunset terrace in the camp, he said to me, "I have a beautiful idea. I want to take a moving picture of Mr. Wright and at the end I would like to take a picture of Mr. Wright's old hands and move my camera to those of some child in whose hands, symbolically illustrated, he will pass on the future of architecture."

I looked at him, wondering, "What has become of his vision of the present?" and turned to him. "But Mr. Wright's hands are young, expressive, beautiful. It seems to me an insult to put the chubby, cute, but inexpressive hands of a child next to his. I do not see beauty in that idea. That is a dissonance to me. If you really want to present beauty in your picture, you should take the chubby, cute but inexpressive hands of a child; then show Mr. Wright's magnificent, creative, superbly intelligent hands, with the motion of which he is changing the face of the world."

The architect looked at me doubtful, still assured of his stand. But he never took the moving picture.

In the nineteen years since this visit, Mr. Wright's hands have been photographed, televised and widely discussed. They have been published as the most expressive and beautiful hands of a creative artist. I wonder what that architect is thinking now?

A film, taken on Mr. Wright's birthday, June 8th, 1958, has been shown on television all over the world. In one hand is his pencil and in the other his T-square, his head bent over his work and his hands moving with a sensitive and precise touch.

His life could not be divided into years. He conceived the vision of a beautiful world. He continued to see buildings, villages, towns, cities of the world, expressing the origin of our spiritual heritage. He built every building to glorify the beauty of the human spirit in terms of stone and steel, wood and brick, glass, plastic and concrete. He made Space come to life in structural form enclosed by walls and roof to enhance and accentuate its interior. He raised man by way of his surroundings and inspired him to live up to the best in himself. The little school Mr. Wright built in Wyoming Valley in Wisconsin will serve as an inspiration that will remain with the children of the Valley throughout the rest of their lives. There is no reason why all schools should not be beautiful, simple in the manner of the Wyoming Valley School. With each building he demonstrated how one can build for practical use without losing sight of beauty.

He saw the cities of the future coming back to take the fresh air of the country. He saw an exodus from overpopulated areas into the land where man can again be called the master of his terrain. The increase of the machine, the automobile and the truck, more and more cramping of livable space, forbids man to partake of his own freedom. Mr. Wright moved ahead urging his people to go with him into the great American spaces where man can live as he once lived in the time of George Washington and Thomas Jefferson—a life of happy exchange with his neighbors, a life at normal pace where an individual could talk truthfully with another.

In this undivided life of his, this spirit and work of his, Mr. Wright stood outside the limits of age, consecrating his life to beauty for all mankind. True to his principle, he moved on always a few paces ahead of his fellow men to show them a great life to be lived by everyone who sees truth as beauty. For truth is beauty, an attribute of Divinity, and can radiate only beauty. So the deeds done against truth serve it just as well. They serve to help the cause, the pursuit and the aim of men dedicated to truth.

There are all kinds of attacks. When Jesus attacked the merchants in the temple, overthrowing their tables of wares, it was for the preservation of the integrity of a temple. There is not one among us who would not justify Jesus for His attack on the trespassers of beauty and principle, which the temple stood for; or for his attack on the Pharisees—the people of learning—for their hypocrisy. But when Jesus was besieged with hatred and insult on His road to Golgotha carrying His cross upon His shoulder, there is not one among us who would not be indignant at the shameful violence inflicted upon Him by the mob.

We stand in awe of His life and His suffering. He is a symbol to us. He who lived according to the supreme ideal: to the spirit of man incarnate in flesh He dedicated His life.

I think of this noble spirit who walked the earth in order to give meaning to our lives, in order to prepare us for a higher destiny; and how many times we fail Him in this attempt to be as He envisioned us—members of a highly evolved society. If we fail Him, we fail God. If we fail our fellow man, we fail God. And if we fail ourselves, we fail God.

Science is taking away from us our ideals. Science is violating the dignity of the human spirit. Science lacks the vision of the prophet; else how could it give to unqualified human beings the secret powers of destruction? If ever there were a contra-position to God, it truly is Satan in the cloak of science. We can only fight it with faith in God and the immortality of the human spirit.

Why should man have so little faith? Why should he apply the standard measure to those it cannot fit? It is fearful to think of the multitude of set barriers over which man climbs up and down only to meet more of them. Faith could dissolve such barriers and the vision of man would then be unimpeded.

But direct perception is difficult to achieve. Too much education, too much "information," too much useless talk, slowly blind man as layers of hard crust grow around him through which he can no longer see.

Mr. Wright accepted everyone and everything. He had not one barrier that stayed any length of time to interfere with his spontaneous, fresh receptivity of the world around him. Nature, to him, was his continuous source of knowledge and delight. He saw into the nature of man with that same swift unimpeded vision and he loved man, notwithstanding man's weaknesses.

Anyone who rises to fame stands out like a mountain. As fame grows, friends increase and in proportion enemies increase. Success is easier to achieve than to maintain. The responsibilities become more involved and the enemies more profuse.

Even with perfect recognition of the fact that we cannot be liked by everyone, we are always shocked to discover that someone does not like us. It seems to be a part of human nature to wish to be appraised correctly, to be respected, and to be loved. Any misjudgment, disrespect, depreciation of ourselves or our work, hurts—though we are fully prepared because we understand that it is a fallacious assumption that we can be liked by everyone. And in this very fact of being hurt by slander lies a kernel of goodness, a desire to share the best within oneself. The pain of slander is the sign of human yearning to create a superior society; a dream society in which each member has respect for the other and works toward betterment for future generations. We wish to pass to them faith in the indestructible integrity of the human spirit. How could we ever achieve it if we did not suffer the pangs of slander? And with the experience of this pain we strive to strengthen and ennoble ourselves, that we may face our Creator without the burden of regret.

It is because of this that the Divine Man said, "Love thine enemies"—the highest and hardest aim to reach. What stature of being it demands! Yet I know that enemies act in ignorance, in misunderstanding, and through accumulation of their own pains and futile frustrations of a life that did not allow them to express the best elements of themselves.

PART TWO

OUR WORK

Chapter 6

FRANK LLOYD WRIGHT'S LETTER
TO THE UNIVERSITY OF WICHITA

In August of 1957 Dean Jackson O. Powell of the University of Wichita in Kansas, asked Mr. Wright to design a model school for their Department of Education. Dean Powell believed that neighborhood schools would become more and more the nucleus of cultural development. He based his belief on the idea that the city is naturally dividing itself into neighborhood units. The school could serve as a nucleus for the cultural life of the community. The teachers would be of higher caliber and would be the leaders of each community.

Mr. Powell's proposed program was well received and endorsed by President Harry F. Corbin under whose advanced leadership this University is rapidly expanding. The University of Wichita is fortunate also in having a group of enlightened and forward looking regents who saw in this proposed scheme a great opportunity to further the work of this modern institution.

This was Mr. Powell's proposed program: Mr. Wright was to design two buildings for the Research Educational Center—the administration building containing classrooms, offices, workrooms and research facilities; and the library for the Department of Education.

149

Mr. Wright designed a circular building surrounding an open court to be a cultural laboratory for the research department in which the teachers will study advanced teaching methods. They will do this by actually conducting a kindergarten and grammar school through the sixth grade for some 250 neighborhood children. Thus the teachers will study teaching methods in actual practice. One side of the elementary school opens into a park which will have special educational and play features for training children in directed play. The buildings are planned with a maximum amount of glass shaded by wide overhangs. The estimated cost is $1,250,000.

The University officials were delighted with Mr. Wright's design. On June 30th, 1959 our chief architect, William Wesley Peters, flew to Kansas to survey the ground and to have a conference with President Corbin, Dean Powell and the regents. Within a week of his return, the Frank Lloyd Wright Foundation was officially directed to proceed with the completion of working drawings.

This had been one of Mr. Wright's favorite projects and naturally it made us feel happy to do this work for a very much needed contribution to the education of the young. What can be more inspiring for the development of the individual than a creative environment in which to study and work? Since not many are given the opportunity to have a beautiful home of their own, it is more than ever necessary to send children to a school which will provide such a creative atmosphere for them as well as for the teachers and the community.

150

Upon the acceptance of his plans, Mr. Wright wrote the following letter:

"May 28th, 1958

"To the University of Wichita

"Gentlemen of the Institution: I wish to record my feeling of grateful appreciation to you all for enthusiastic acceptance of my design for the Administration and Classroom buildings which I have made at your request.

"Architecture is, I believe, the corner-stone of any indigenous culture that will bear the brand American —and it is 'Education' that has most neglected this fundamental feature of our cultural foundation. For too long a time Education has subscribed to the standard brands (Gothic for instance), to the sophistications of the Paris Beaux Arts. Neither course has been able to inculcate or discover the American Spirit. *We* build *our* national life upon Sovereignty of the Individual. The old styles become definitely dated, useful only to those unable to accept the freedom of thought and action implied by our Declaration.

"But American Architecture was first to realize the new opportunity as a great obligation and dig deeper for the forms our new life should take. Naturally the new forms would have a character of beauty beyond anything heretofore known because now the Freedom of Man—his soul competent—could only result in new ways of building to accord with our new free-thought and consequent changing waves of being.

"Well, our American Universities were not first in seeing this nor helping it come to pass in Architecture. Fruits of an organic architecture for America—the only

151

architecture true to it—have been too long controversial, if in fact receiving intelligent attention at all.

"Like Government, Education has known only cowardice where this radical law of change was concerned. The East was too far gone to even see the need of it. The Middle West saw it but shied away toward 'Gothic.' The Far West was more free to act, but 'knew not where to go.'

"But of late years, the movement toward so-called 'modern' has gone far and wide as merely a left-wing of original organic architecture. Therefore it is the more timely and encouraging that Middle West Wichita has made this world-notable subscription to what can, without equivocation, be called 'American Architecture.'

"In behalf of young lives deeply involved in this Wichita decision the country can only be grateful for a much-needed exemplar of the truth of romance in Architecture, as in all other forms of human *being* according to Nature.

"Furthermore, it is this architect's fond hope that all goes well with the venture—most needed on the part of Education—and all comes to the happy conclusion that 769 buildings of similar parentage have found.

"May reward for your perspicacity and courage, so uncommon in this realm of Education, come to all of you concerned with your architect in adding to evidence of an American culture of our own."

—Frank Lloyd Wright

Chapter 7

FELLOWSHIP

In the buildings represented by the winners of the competition sponsored by the American Institute of Architects in 1959 I saw not one valid original idea in the use of either forms or materials. I saw fragments of Mr. Wright's influence but always distorted, always devoid of the quality that makes his architecture vibrant with life.

In the winners' designs I discerned not only a composite of Mr. Wright's architecture, but of the Greek —columns pared down to square forms or fragments of Romanesque architecture—combined with the utter bareness called the International Style.

On the other hand, the design by William Wesley Peters, of our Taliesin Associated Architects, for a mortuary in Delano, California, shows such a knowledge of the principles of structure and such artistic perception that it stands above comparison with the designs of the contemporary winners.

It is an exciting building. The star-shaped plan is very simple and harmonious. Each point of the star which surrounds the circular central chapel seating 158 people embodies a particular function: the family wing, music chamber, reception hall, storage space for flowers, lodge and pallbearers' rooms—all are triangles which form the star. On one side many of these rooms open onto enclosed gardens.

The building, made of concrete block, glass and sheet metal, has charm and poetry wedded to practical utility. The chapel has a truly religious feeling. The ceiling of the interior central hall is supported by wooden trusses interwoven with globe-shaped lights. During the day it will be lit through high clerestory windows wrapped around the ceiling which changes in height as its levels recede. On one side the circular wall is perforated in a gentle pattern to transmit freely the sound of music pouring into the chapel.

The whole impression is that of continuity, creating a meditative, reflective atmosphere.

This quality of artistic perception combined with knowledge of structure exists in various degrees in the work of all those who adhere to the principles of organic architecture exalted in the work of Mr. Wright, and frankly declare so. It is because of this that their buildings bear the mark of strength and sincerity. They do not hide behind the false fronts of forced deviation which only quasi-intellectuals can call "originality." They design outright and build with fundamental understanding of the work before them.

The advanced minds of today call Frank Lloyd Wright the greatest architect who ever lived. His ideas are based on the principles of organic architecture which means that they apply to any time and any land, the basic principle being to blend with nature, architecture—integral with nature—in its noblest form.

It is obvious that any foolish attempt to violate life and to force "new" forms in a frustrated wish for originality is distortion of the principle. A great architecture seldom comes into the world. We are fortunate that Mr. Wright had prepared a nucleus of architects electrified by the great principle, who will keep the crystalline purity of it, and will therefore, in every building they build, cherish the life of that building. Then architecture will continue to live as a great art.

With the exception of our big flower Triangle beside the highway leading up to Taliesin in Wisconsin, our gardens that same summer of 1959 were perfected everywhere by our very possessive lovers of flowers. Devotion to their individual gardens practically obliterated the great Triangle which had been our pride for many years. So I took a rather strong hand and, stopping all the activities of Taliesin, sent everyone to the Triangle to clear it of weeds.

"You," I said to Bruce Brooks Pfeiffer, "have made yourself a veritable Versailles garden at Tan-y-deri. Not one but four of them! With luxuriant perennials and annuals, and delicious scents floating in the air. You have decorated your gardens with flawless geometric borders drawn as by a compass. Your lawns are as smooth as the shell of an egg—and all the while you criminally neglected the Triangle."

"You," I said to Shirley Casey of the Forest House, "made yourself a copious, luscious English garden, with flowers blooming from around the corners of each shrub, woodpile and dump in the backyard! You even wedged flowers in the woods themselves—while you criminally neglected the Triangle on the highway."

"You," I said to Cornelia Brierly of Midway, "have made yourself an Italian villa atmosphere of hanging baskets and window boxes, with flowers falling off the banks in cascades. Even the stone steps lead through elevated platforms in a triumphant procession of colors —while you let the big Triangle on the highway go to weed!"

"You," I said to John Rattenbury of the Westwing, "have made yourself a palatial grass terrace, surrounded with abundant flowers of myriads of color and shades shimmering in the sun. You ran your prolific priceless portulaca all the way down twenty feet to make your pathway toward Westwing a spectacle of glory! And you were not satisfied with the common variety of portulaca—oh, no! Not you, Sir John R.! You had to have the exotic kind, double, triple, quadruple layers of brilliantly shaded petals are your portulaca. Not one weed, not even a blade of grass among them. And look at the Triangle on the highway—you can hardly find the flowers!"

"And all of you, the Fellowship!" I said. "All of you kept promising me daily, 'We will fix it up tomorrow, Mrs. Wright'—and one tomorrow turned into another, without change. I no longer believe you. Drop everything and go to the Triangle. Don't leave it until you have pulled out every weed!"

I joined them in the big push, and the Triangle on the highway was cleaned of weeds. As we pulled the weeds out, we found that they had occupied such large spaces that we had to bring in more plants. The owners of the luxuriant gardens volunteered on their own to dig up flowers from their gardens and fill the empty places.

Little Shirley Casey of the Forest House hauled six truckloads from her garden; Bruce Brooks Pfeiffer, three from his; John Rattenbury, the most—eight truckloads!

I could not believe it. We planted them early in the morning and we planted after supper. The garden ate them all and still there were bare spots. The sun beat down mercilessly during the day and we worried about the flowers surviving the heat.

Looking at those young people who had sacrificed their flowers, I began to feel badly. When they volunteered to bring more I thought I detected sadness in their eyes. With my heart rather uneasy, I got into my car to see the plundered gardens. But for the life of me I could find no place where the flowers had been dug out! If anything, their gardens looked even more luxuriant than ever. I joked about it with them and they agreed.

But I did not want them to dig more and we decided to send Ling Po to Mineral Point, twenty miles away, to bring back some bright geraniums, salvia, marigolds, or whatever he could find. Ling Po left at three that afternoon and said he would bring them back long before supper time so that we could continue to plant. Aubrey Banks was hauling water in a big tank on the pickup truck and pumping it into the garden. All of us were muddy, covered with streaks of dirt, weeding out the last of the obstinate weeds while waiting for Ling Po.

The message came to the Triangle that Ling Po had driven to Dubuque, Iowa, sixty miles away . . . Sorry, but will be back at eight o'clock . . .

We continued working and watching for Ling Po. Eight o'clock passed by . . . nine o'clock passed by . . . it became dark. No Ling Po.

At ten we went up to the house and had some refreshments. I told everyone to give up the work; we would plant the following morning.

"No," John R. said. "We would rather wait. The flowers will do better if we plant them tonight."

I went in. They told me in the morning that Ling Po arrived at 10:45.

What had happened to Ling Po?

Not finding flowers in Mineral Point, his spirit undaunted, he drove to Dubuque, Iowa. Finding none there, he stubbornly pursued his search and drove to Galena, Illinois, seventy miles away. Again finding no red flowers, he drove to Monroe, Wisconsin, forty-five miles away, where he was finally victorious and returned with twenty flats of red geraniums. Ling Po has his Chinese relentless persistence. I knew that if there were one last flat of flowers left in the state of Wisconsin and the adjoining states, he would locate it!

The young people planted all of them by car headlights and railway torches. The personal pride in their personal gardens was transferred now to the Triangle.

We had invited the editorial staff of the *Capital Times* and their wives to be our guests on that Saturday for dinner. Naturally, we were eager to show ourselves at our best. Whole groups of us now walked around the Triangle with gasps of admiration—to us the garden was sheer beauty, perfection and wonder. And when Editor Evjue arrived at Taliesin I quickly took him to the windows of our living room and said, "Mr. Evjue, isn't the Triangle garden beautiful?"

He looked at me and said firmly, "There are lots of empty spots in that garden since you pulled out the weeds."

"Empty spots?" I asked, genuinely shocked. "There are no empty spots—we filled them all with flowers!"

"Well," he said relentlessly, "that garden was beautiful last year. It was solidly covered with flowers."

"But Mr. Evjue! Let us drive down. I'll show you that there are no empty spots."

He swept two-year old Derice Pfefferkorn from her mother's arms, carried her to the car and we drove to the Triangle.

"Look," I said, "where are the empty spots? You see, it is all covered with flowers."

I drove by very slowly—around and around.

"Well," he said, "it looks better from here . . . but last year . . . gee, it was really beautiful."

"What is the use?" I thought dejectedly and drove back to Taliesin just in time to welcome my colleagues and their charming wives. Dinner was served on the grass terrace outside the theater foyer where we could watch the sun redden the sky, and the hills gently sink into dusk.

The motion picture that evening was *Oh Men, Oh Women,* a comedy which we had seen two weeks before and thought very funny as well as constructive in its theme. It was chosen after long deliberation, believing that our guests might enjoy relaxing at the end of a hot summer day. We were glad to hear a burst of laughter here and there but many of us worried that they might not have thought the picture as funny as we had.

That night the rain came down in torrents and on Sunday there was a Mother-of-Pearl-cast sky—cool and lovely for the flowers. And Monday the rain kept falling with a tender touch. And on Tuesday, heavy, delightful fog descended on our Valley. The flowers all recovered from their fainting spell and stood there smiling and growing in silent bond with us.

John H. Howe, the chief of the Taliesin drafting room, came to study architecture twenty-seven years ago when we had barely begun the work with a handful of young people. There is no one—I would say, in the world—that can match the output and capacity of John Howe. He is virtually a wizard at drafting. He worked alongside Mr. Wright for so long that he could delineate Mr. Wright's plans practically in one breath!

With the help of his devoted wife, Lu, John built for them a cottage at Taliesin, on a nearby hill, working on it quietly for several years.

It is in the nature of a miracle to me to see that charming little structure high on the hill. The whole house is the size of an average living room, yet it has a sense of spaciousness, an atmosphere of warmth and friendliness. The little bedroom is compact—everything in it occupies its legitimate place and gives the feeling of effortless comfort.

John and Lu have worked side by side, faithfully and steadily—he in his tremendous contribution in the drafting room, she in her capable secretarial work. Lu, too, is swift and precise, and can produce more than anyone that has ever been in that capacity at Taliesin. She also weaves beautiful fabrics of her husband's design and, with her gaiety and style, presents a lovely picture in our social life.

We of course place great emphasis on gracious relationships with one another and in a gracious attitude toward any guest who might take pleasure in our entertainment. We believe that life is integral and that one cannot separate one part as less important than another. We believe that we cannot live just for the sake of accumulating money in order to do, one day, the things that we have always wanted to do. We believe that one can fulfill some of these desires modestly, right along with working and living in accordance to what the budget permits.

There has never been a time at Taliesin when we let down our social life. When we had practically no clients and hardly any income, when Mr. Wright and I devoted every effort of our life to maintaining the Fellowship, even then we still kept the social aspects of our life uninterrupted.

I often claim that, no matter how small the budget, everyone can do that. And the saving of money, although important indeed, must be done in proper measure so that the best years of one's life are not missed by constant anxiety and worry of the future. Because the future is with us now and we should do with it the best we can.

In addition to the steady group always working in the drafting room, we have various projects assigned to other groups until their turn comes to join the drafting room work. It has frequently been our experience that the young people are so devoted to some project outside that it is hard to get them back into the drafting room, even those who are just beginning to study architectural drawing. The Meadow Farm was one such project. At first they went rather reluctantly to work at the Meadow Farm, three miles away from Taliesin, but when I drove there three weeks later, I found at least a dozen cars parked on the lawn and the work going at full pitch.

Mr. Wright bought the Meadow Farm back in 1957 because we needed more room for our apprentices. He told me then that I could repair the little house. We now attacked that work with such zest as only we know. And the dilapidated house with its rotting floors, sagging walls, cracked concrete, broken windows, began slowly to take on a fresh look. The interest and excitement aroused over the Meadow Farm grew daily.

Marshall Erdman, the Madison contractor, was kind enough to let us hire his prized carpenter, Mr. Richgels of Madison. The apprentices appreciated Mr. Richgels' fine craftsmanship and the swiftness of the strokes of his hammer. They were in awe of his achievement and I noticed that more and more young people were flocking to the Meadow Farm to help this excellent and friendly craftsman. I believe the appreciation was mutual in the sense of love of work because Mr. Richgels gave freely of his time. As a matter of fact Mr. Erdman was forced to telephone in distress: "You asked for Mr. Richgels for only three days," he said. "You now have had him over a week. I must have him back. He likes it so much over there, but he is my foreman—I can spare him no longer!"

So the romance between Mr. Richgels and the Fellowship had to come to an end.

The feverish pace at the Meadow Farm continued almost all summer. My problem was how to stop our young people from installing another window in another corner, from knocking out another wall leading to another terrace, from putting another concrete platfrom on the other side, from re-designing the ceiling and adding more and more and more shelves. At the Meadow Farm they were—to use Mr. Wright's favorite expression—"like hungry orphans turned loose in a bake shop."

Arnold Roy from Massachusetts, who has been with us over seven years, works like a flash of lightning. I believe he designs and builds faster than anyone in the world. Combined with his speed his craftsmanship is flawless and the results are miraculous. Mr. Wright often said, "That boy is a wizard."

So Arnold had to be watched very carefully, otherwise he would try to put into execution his good but frequently extravagant ideas. He was so upset one day when he learned that I had decided not to buy new doors for the downstairs rooms that without asking me he drove to Dodgeville and bought the doors himself!

Cornelia Brierly made frequent trips into Madison, visiting second-hand stores, triumphantly returning with stove, ice box, washing machine, rugs and china ware. And with what a thrill she was received: a dozen young people always rushed to the truck to unload the various bargains, admiring the china ware and its pretty patterns, and "a rug which has not even a spot on it."

But when they wanted to build a fireplace in the living room, I really had to say "no." Without my knowledge they got a Heatilator from our client, Seth Peterson, of our neighboring town, Black Earth.

"Were we to buy one it would cost at least $75," they said.

"We will build it into the fireplace with cement blocks. It will warm four rooms," Kenn Lockhart explained enthusiastically.

"How much will this cost?" I asked.

Cornelia Brierly, who submitted the design for the fireplace, replied too promptly, "We figured it out exactly. It will cost us $80."

I looked away. "And how long will it take you to wreck this wall and insert the fireplace?" I pressed.

Kenn hesitated, "A week—or a little more."

I knew better.

"No," I said. "No fireplace this year. Store the Heatilator in the machine shop. We may build it in the spring."

They all sighed and looked ruefully at their Heatilator.

I could not help but feel pleased at their eagerness to come as close to perfection as possible.

Love of work is a rare gift, dependent entirely upon the spirit of man. The higher the development of the spirit, the deeper the love of work. Loving work for its own sake, no matter how minute the contribution, provides a release from one's own limitations. Fortunate indeed is the one who possesses this gift.

The members of the Taliesin Fellowship worked

hard through the difficult summer of 1959, attacking one job after another. Taking care of the drafting room, the plans, the working drawings and the new designs consumed all their time.

I had placed Kenn Lockhart in charge of the Meadow Farm construction and Cornelia Brierly supervised the interior decorating. It took much longer than I had thought to repair and make changes in the little house. We were there daily, but the work seemed to move very slowly. I decided to set a deadline.

"Next Sunday," I said, "we will have the house-warming at Meadow Farm. The house must be finished, all the rooms completed, including the flower arrangements on the table and the shelves. We will sod the grounds so it will appear as though nothing had been disturbed during the construction."

Our farmer, Bill Logue, suggested that we roast on the spit four suckling pigs which he had saved and kept in deep freeze.

We invited Mrs. Barney, Mr. Evjue, the neighboring friends and farmers, and the master-carpenter, Mr. Richgels and his wife, to join us for the house-warming.

In order to show the way to the Meadow Farm, I asked John Amarantides to build a sign based on the theme of a four-leaf clover and alfalfa blossom. When Mr. Evjue, Mrs. Barney and I drove up to the gate, John had finished the sign to which Eugene Masselink pointed, "You see, there is a four-leaf clover and there is alfalfa."

But I could see neither. Some squarish planes of wood headed the lettering and a string of triangles hung on one side! But it was beautiful whatever it was, and the words "Meadow Farm" were carved in a distinguished way.

Colorful streamers floated from poles, cheerful and gay, and decorations of Japanese lanterns were strung on branches of the trees; the concrete steps and gravel walk led us to the little house. Everything looked so quiet there and our young people as hosts were so gracious that no one, not even Mr. Evjue, would have suspected the rush, the pressure, the flashes of temperament that had taken place just a short while before.

The four pigs were roasting on the spit. It was a picturesque sight—men stripped to the waist, constantly turning the spit, their faces shimmering with lights and shadows of the flames. The evening was soft and reflective. Children ran and played in the green meadows.

We sat down on the concrete terrace in front of the house; music drifted in the air and a lovely locust tree, called Saint John's bread, hung right over our heads. The hills in the distance were semi-circular against the sky; the clouds above them were drawn in horizontal, almost straight lines. Of course Mrs. Barney immediately saw them *all* embroidered with yarn on her felt!

We went upstairs to see Bill Owen's display of his great work of interior decorating: in that tiny room of his, just seven by twelve feet, he had crammed more shelves than I thought it capable of consuming. But strangely enough, the room took it, including a display of stained glass covering five vertical light fixtures. Our guests were delighted with Bill's work and he naturally glowed with pleasure.

We finally settled to the feast and everyone exclaimed over the juiciness of the meat; those with sound digestive tracts ate the luscious, savory brown skin while the rest of us watched them in helpless envy.

After the picnic we went to the Taliesin Playhouse to see a comedy film. Tired though we all were from the day's hectic activities, the picture was entertaining, at times touching. There was laughter that for a short while released the tension and pressure of our work.

Chapter 8

THE GARDEN

The very last sketch Mr. Wright drew was for an enclosed garden for me. To give us both some peace and seclusion he planned it so that it was to be removed from the general activity. I had asked him for a long time to have a garden such as that. And the very first thing I did after the June 8th Memorial Dinner was to have his design carried out.

When the Taliesin perfectionists started to work on my garden walls, Nari Gandhi from Bombay appraised every rock, no matter how small, for its aesthetic fitness. He painstakingly chose the color of the rock, lovingly turning it this way and that until, finally when his own sense of proportion was satisfied, he used it in the wall. He carved each rock with the understanding of a craftsman and with the love and tenderness of an artist.

He inspired all others who worked with him and raised them to the level of his perfection. I believe that the walls of my garden must be the most beautiful walls in the world. Daily I watched the bent heads of the young apprentices and the mason, Ralph Nowatney from the Valley, cutting the stone with them. I saw our

168

venerable mason, George Haas of Spring Green, whose work Mr. Wright always praised highly, coming daily to sit in a chair in the sun amid flying rocks and dust to direct all of the work. Because he had suffered a heart attack the previous fall, Mr. Haas directed the work without laying the rocks himself. And who could be more qualified to supervise the building of the stone walls than he? For fifteen years he had been fashioning the most beautiful masonry at Taliesin and Hillside. George Haas has taught numerous Taliesin students how to cut rock, and how to lay it with masterly, flawless craftsmanship.

It was gratifying to see him sitting there giving counsel on the length of the rocks to be laid deep in the ground, and the rising of the wall with handsome coping stones to finish its line.

The walls were growing—bathed in care and love— very, very slowly. Every day, surrounded by enthusiastic young faces, I watched its progress. They showed me the latest rock or at best the latest patch of rock that composed the wall, and all the beauties that were to follow. I simply had no heart to ask when it was to be finished.

It took them several months to do this extraordinary work, but after all my garden walls are 8 feet high and 240 feet long!

Perfection has its price, as everything of quality does. While watching this painstaking labor of love I was reminded of an incident in my own life.

My old friend Jeanne deSalzmann worked with me in the Institute of Fontainebleau-Avon. We were both students of philosophy and there too we did all the work ourselves. Jeanne deSalzmann came to visit us a few years ago at Taliesin and told Mr. Wright how she and I were assigned the job of hauling stones in wheel barrows from a rock pile to the buildings of a new addition.

"You know what happened?" she said laughingly. "Every time we wheeled our wheel barrows to the rock pile, I would load mine quickly and be ready to go. But Olgivanna annoyed me terribly. Not only would she choose the rocks carefully and put just the ones she liked into her wheel barrow, but after they were in, she would keep rearranging them in such a way that the best ones would be on top. In addition to that, she would roll some over so that the most beautiful lichen-covered surface would show. And every time we pushed the wheel barrows to the building, we would be terribly scolded because we were too slow. Of course I never told on Olgivanna," she laughed freely.

Mr. Wright was more pleased than I expected. As a matter of fact he was pleased beyond what I deserved. He even went so far as to say that was why our marriage was successful! I believe this reaction was quite incomprehensible to my friend.

Chapter 9

THE GUGGENHEIM MUSEUM

In 1939 Mr. Wright received a telegram from Solomon R. Guggenheim who wanted a building for his large collection of modern art, inviting him to come to New York for a conference regarding a new museum. That was a lean year for Taliesin and we were glad of the good news of a good job. Mr. Wright and I took the next train to New York.

Noble, gentlemanly Mr. Guggenheim invited us to his apartment at the Plaza where he discussed with Mr. Wright his ideas for a new type of building to be erected on Fifth Avenue. Both men liked one another and from that first meeting until Mr. Guggenheim's death they remained the kind of friends who always had a good time together. He and his wife were both a pleasure to be with. At the age of seventy-five Mrs. Guggenheim had a beautiful classic face. The touch of time always remained in her eyes.

They invariably entertained us lavishly. Mr. Guggenheim was delighted with the non-objective paintings solidly covering the walls of his apartment, turning it into an art gallery. He explained to me in detail the beauty of geometric forms which sometimes were so

sparse that a canvas four feet high and eight feet wide
would contain just three small, vaguely triangular figures. I was dumbfounded while listening to him. "You
see, this is only to emphasize space," he said with a
gentle smile. "The figures in themselves have no meaning except as they make you conscious of space."

I nodded my head without understanding—staring
into white canvas, desperately trying to feel "space."
Fortunately, he moved me to the next non-objective
painting. When he came to the painter, Wassily Kandin-
sky, I breathed more easily because I could appreciate
the play and fusion of lovely color.

Our most gracious host was in love with his collection
of paintings which were his bequest to the culture of
the future.

Mr. Wright appreciated the architecture and the atmosphere of the Plaza Hotel. He had high esteem for
Henry Hardenburg, the architect, and thought his work
had style. He was shocked by the way the hotel was
treated by modern remodelers, and was appalled by
the removal of the frescoes in the lobby and the destruction caused by the closing of the once beautiful
glass ceiling of the Palm Court. He went several times
to the manager to ask him not to carpet the Italian
marble mosaic floor of the lobbies, and was happy to
see the rugs removed during the summer months. Mr.
Wright was eager to preserve the old beauty that had
dignity and elegance.

He remembered that the mirrored doors at the back
of the Palm Court had once connected with the ball-
room. He asked our son-in-law, Wesley Peters, to open

them, one evening, and it was lovely to behold the space undivided. But the management closed them again.

Whenever we were seated for lunch in the Edwardian Room Mr. Wright never failed to point out to me the beauty of the painted ceiling. We occasionally went to the Persian Room which originally was decorated by Joseph Urban, his colleague and friend. The paintings had been removed and Mr. Wright expressed his disappointment every time we ate dinner there.

We so frequently stayed at the Plaza ourselves that we decided to rent an apartment at the hotel since there was need for an office when our work began to concentrate in the East. We chose a suite on the second floor which Mr. Wright redesigned and completely refurnished—capturing and bringing to life the vanishing spirit of elegance. He interpreted the old style of the building in new terms which were sympathetic to the past.

On the walls he placed panels of Japanese gold paper surrounded by a rose colored border. He mounted circular mirrors within the semi-circular window arches, making them a part of the window, with long cord pendants with crystal balls attached to them with which to turn on the lights behind the mirrors. Long red velvet curtains hung almost directly from the high ceiling. In the meantime at Taliesin, several apprentices built tables, easels and seats which Mr. Wright had designed for the new apartment. Painted with black lacquer and red edges, they were handsome and practical.

Finally, the furniture arrived at the Plaza and we worked all day to establish order because we had invited clients for dinner. David Dodge, one of our apprentices, was putting the last strokes of black paint on the fireplace when the guests began to ring the door bell . . .

The Taliesin atmosphere of work permeated the apartment for five years until January 27, 1959—the last time we were there.

William Short, the superintendent of the Guggenheim Museum, and a few others carefully packed the furniture of the apartment and a truck brought it to Taliesin. This furniture now graces our Forest House in Wisconsin a mile from Taliesin, giving it a touch of elegance. Looking out of the Forest House windows I can see the smooth lawn, maple trees and pines. I also see Central Park, Fifth Avenue and 59th Street. I hear our Wisconsin meadow larks and cardinals, robins and mourning doves. I also hear the pigeons outside on the sill of the Plaza windows—forever cooing and fighting each other. I hear Mr. Wright saying, "Look at that speckled pigeon—he is the boss—the rest are afraid of him." And we watch him first strut on the thin iron rail, then take off for flight over the traffic signals among the blackened skyscrapers . . .

Many lives within us for a time run parallel to one another, later to be fused until there is no separation.

During those years at the Plaza Mr. Wright and I frequently drove to the Guggenheims' palatial mansion in Port Washington to stay a day or two with them. It was an enormous estate. The house was a veritable old palace with wide carpeted stairways, great reception

174

rooms, halls, tall ceilings, terraces—all on a magnificent scale. When walking through those endless rooms, one felt in the vast spaces a sense of loneliness and regret for a life that was and could no longer be. But when we gathered in the dining room with its shimmering, lighted candelabra, the atmosphere came to life. It became warm and friendly.

At the table one evening, Mr. Wright spoke of the Russians: "Don't you know that the Russians are really Mongolians? They are all descendants of Genghis Khan. Look at them—their cheek bones are high, the whole structure betrays their Mongolian origin."

"But," I interrupted, "they are of fair skin, blue eyes, golden hair. Their noses are upturned, their . . ."

Mr. Wright stopped me. "That is just a thin strip— most of the Russians are Mongolians."

Mr. Guggenheim turned to me with a sparkle in his eyes, "If we don't watch out, he is going to make redskinned Indians out of us all!"

And while we were talking the butler came in and carried my plate away unfinished. "He is awfully fast," Mr. Guggenheim remarked. "Next time, keep your hand on your plate if you want to eat in this house!"

I remember the day when the plans of the museum were presented to Mr. Guggenheim. He stretched out his hand to shake Mr. Wright's and with tears in his eyes said, "This is it. This is what I wanted. You are the only man who could have done it."

Such complete approval was inspiring to Mr. Wright —and it brought the two still closer together.

The following years were spent on working drawings

and when they were completed, the bids satisfactory, the economic state of the country interfered with the project; Solomon R. Guggenheim waited for the recession. Years went rolling along with no recession in sight, but Mr. Guggenheim said he was a patient man —he would wait—he had seen the 1929 depression when prices fell and "you could build a building practically for a song." More years moved into the past. Mr. Guggenheim waited. The year 1949 arrived—still no recession. Solomon R. Guggenheim became fatally ill that year and died without seeing the most beautiful museum in the world, which his initiative had brought into existence.

His nephew, Harry Guggenheim, became the President of the Board of Trustees of the Solomon R. Guggenheim Foundation. Requests for changes began, more work, more years, more changes. Mr. Wright never lost faith that the building would be built notwithstanding many a "wise man's" dramatic prophecy to the contrary. With confidence Harry Guggenheim competently pressed on while requesting more changes and what appeared to be endless work for Mr. Wright and our entire staff. Finally—after a series of long discussions and complex conferences to and fro—the actual construction started in 1956.

In November of 1958 when Mr. Wright and I saw the museum it was almost finished except for the last decisions and the last touches, the last struggles against the wrong changes . . . He saw his building, hard fought for, standing on Fifth Avenue—a symbol of the spirit of independence, freedom and democracy.

In the year of 1959, President Harry Guggenheim

and the Trustees of the Solomon R. Guggenheim Foundation began making arrangements for the opening. Mr. Guggenheim sent me the following program: Monday, October nineteenth, a preview for the press and art critics from two to six p.m., dinner at the home of Mr. and Mrs. Guggenheim with the Trustees, then to the reception at the Museum for artists and architects. The following evening: a dinner with the officials who were to take part in the opening ceremonies, then on to the Museum where a reception was to be held for friends and distinguished guests from nine to twelve p.m.

At the official ceremonies on Wednesday the twenty-first at noon, Secretary Flemming of the United States Department of Health, Education and Welfare was to deliver the main address and read a letter from President Eisenhower; Ambassador Lodge, Mayor Wagner and Park Commissioner Robert Moses were to participate in the ceremonies. Federal, state and city officials, ambassadors to Washington with their cultural attaches, museum presidents, etc., were also to attend.

Accompanied by my daughter, Iovanna, Eugene Masselink, and Wesley Peters, I flew to New York to attend all the occasions.

Sunday the eighteenth was a mild sunny day and the inhabitants of New York City took their last splurge in the country. Senator and Mrs. William Benton sent their car for us. We drove through a taffy-pulling string of automobiles from the Plaza Hotel, until we finally reached their home in Southport, Connecticut. Helen Benton, our beautiful hostess, greeted us with her husband on the garden lawn in front of their house. Their

177

son, John, a student at Yale, and my grandson Brandoch, a student at the Juilliard School of Music, went happily together toward the surf.

Through the years Helen Benton has been a greatly admired friend of ours. "Not only is she beautiful," Mr. Wright often said, "but so lovely as a person." He was always happy to be in her presence and she was his devoted friend. Since April 9th Helen Benton, in a deep sense, never left my side. Wherever her world travels took her she continued an uninterrupted contact with me. Mr. and Mrs. Benton had recently returned from a two months' cruise on a yacht in Europe. The cruise had started at Lisbon and they had picked up friends at various ports on the Mediterranean—letting off one party, boarding another. Mr. Benton stocked the library of the yacht with books on history and travel, and asked all the guests to study them in reference to the present political, economic and cultural state of each city they visited. With them was their old friend, Adlai Stevenson. It was interesting to hear the impressions of their trip.

At lunch we discussed the America First Organization, which Mr. Benton had disbanded on the day of Pearl Harbor. On that memorable day he had lunch with General Wood, Chairman of the Board of Sears, Roebuck and Company. Mr. Benton asked General Wood how the Encyclopedia Britannica (then owned by Sears, Roebuck) was going—he had heard it was losing money.

General Wood answered briefly that it made $300,-000.00 in the last year. "How would you like to give the Encyclopedia Britannica to the University of Chicago?"

Mr. Benton asked boldly. After three or four questions —which took no longer than three or four minutes— General Wood said, "I'll give you the Encyclopedia Britannica." It was hard for William Benton to believe his ears. He went home and had his friend, Robert Hutchins, who was then the President of the University of Chicago, call General Wood to confirm what had taken place.

"Yes," answered General Wood. "I gave him the Britannica. I have the papers before me. All he has to do is pay $300,000.00 to cover the inventory. The plates and everything else he can have for nothing."

William Benton then turned the Encyclopedia Britannica into a powerful institution, probably the greatest source of reference in the world.

Charles and Anne Lindbergh joined us for coffee. Mr. Lindbergh looked very young in spite of slightly greying hair; she, as usual, very simple and pretty. Anne Lindbergh likes to talk about her cooking for the family and about her care of the children. When I asked, "Are they not all grown by now?," it was he who answered with pride, "We have grandchildren." Neither of them looks like a grandparent.

We drove back to New York in the late afternoon, reaching the Plaza in time for dinner.

On the day of the opening of the Museum for the press, artists and architects, we had lunch with Celia Peabody in her smart apartment on 58th Street just two blocks from the Plaza. She, too, had been on the cruise with the William Bentons and she, too, was full of pleasant reminiscences. "The most instructive trip I have taken in my life," she said.

179

Then back to the Plaza for tea with Joe Price, the son of Mr. and Mrs. Harold Price. He had just returned from India and Lebanon. It seems all our friends were away that summer.

After interviewing a young applicant to the Fellowship who had come all the way from Israel to join our work, we hastily dressed for dinner and the first reception for the press at the Museum.

Mr. and Mrs. Guggenheim's town house is four-story, black and trimmed with white. The rooms were filled with people when we arrived. It was pleasant to see again the Earl Castle Stewart and his wife, daughter of Solomon R. Guggenheim, who had flown from London for the opening. Mr. Wright and I had visited them in London some years before. The Earl Castle Stewart is a poised, pleasant Englishman and his wife is vivacious and spirited in manner.

The Trustees of the Solomon R. Guggenheim Foundation and their wives seemed to have met for the first time at this occasion. There were constant introductions accompanied by the words, "Oh, I have heard so much about you."

Among the guests was William Short, who during all the construction of the Museum, adhered strictly and devotedly to Mr. Wright's designs. He is a Princetonian, gentle, but very persistent in the meticulous execution of his work. It is always gratifying to see such a dedicated and capable young man with faith in an ideal.

Carl Zigrosser and his wife were there. He, too, is one of the Trustees. Distinguished, scholarly Mr.

Zigrosser, a writer and critic, spoke softly of his admiration for Mr. Wright and his work.

Harry Guggenheim was in high spirit. At dinner he said, "I believe Mr. Wright to be a great man, a great genius. I did my best to preserve the integrity of his building. And in my heart here," he put his hand on his breast, "I feel in clear conscience that I have done it, that the building is exactly the way Mr. Wright created it. I worked for it and I fought for it. In some details of the interior I had to follow Museum Director Sweeney's suggestions. I felt that to be his right since he is the Director. But when the trustees change, when the directors change, the interior can be restored at any time to Mr. Wright's exact design. I consider that part an unimportant change that can be done any time. I believe this building to be beautiful, extraordinary, a great work of art." There was earnestness and conviction in Harry Guggenheim's voice.

Our party drove up to the Museum in several cars. The miracle on Fifth Avenue stood as a spirit from another world, glowing with golden bands of light moving upward in an ever-widening spiral.

Preceding the second opening of the Museum—this time for friends and distinguished guests—there was another dinner with Harry and Alicia Guggenheim. On my left sat United States Ambassador Henry Cabot Lodge of the United Nations. Powerfuly built, with much inner vitality, Mr. Lodge was most eloquent. "I am not an architect but I must say there has been too much glass used in the latest buildings erected in New York City. The United Nations Building, as you know, is of much glass. We are building the Headquarters for the American delegation of the United Nations opposite it and this building is going to be of stone."

"Did you dictate that?" I asked.

"I certainly did," he answered positively. "I think we have overdone the use of glass. I am glad your husband's museum is of concrete. It is very refreshing to see it on the Avenue."

"I admire the way you carried your part of the job with Khrushchev," I said. "I watched you on television. It must have been very trying."

"It was," he answered gustily, "Khrushchev went to bed at midnight every night while I had to write the report to the President after every occasion. I seldom went to bed before three or four in the morning."

But Mr. Lodge looked very healthy indeed. "Did you yourself choose your political career?" I asked.

"It is the tradition of my family. I always was interested in social and political affairs. That has been my life work."

"What do you like to do for relaxation?" I asked.

"I love boating. I love the water—that is my favorite form of rest."

On the other side of Mr. Lodge sat our hostess, Alicia, and on her left was Robert Moses.

"Both Mr. Wright and Mr. Moses were great fighters," she drew me into the conversation.

"Yes," I said, "they were—but they need not have fought each other."

Robert Moses smiled, looking down as though embarrassed.

"But it was in fun," Alicia Patterson said, lightening

the tension. "They fought in fun. They were devoted to each other."

"I don't know," I kept my ground. "Why did they not save their energy to fight evil instead of fighting each other?"

Robert Moses smiled, looking uncertain, while Henry Lodge seemed to be quite interested in the cross-table repartee.

Alicia's lovely brown eyes looked at me pleadingly. "It was all in fun between them."

"It was not fun," I persisted, and turning to Robert Moses, "you were responsible for that bad article in the *New York Times* early last summer. I will never forgive you for that—it was the wrong timing."

"You will forgive me," he said with a smile. "You cannot hold a grudge."

"This time I cannot forgive—that was a serious offense."

Alicia Patterson again made light of it. "You know you believe in forgiving."

"Yes, if it were an injury done in ignorance but it is hard to forgive an injury inflicted by an intelligent man."

Robert Moses still repeated, "Olgivanna is going to forgive me."

Henry Lodge listened to the three of us with a bemused expression on his face. This dinner conversation was an almost incomprehensible experience in his diplomatic career!

R. Sturgis Ingersoll, President of the Philadelphia Museum of Fine Art, who sat on my right, spoke to me about his love of books. "If you permit me to be impertinent," he bowed, "I understand your husband did not like books. He did not like to read. He never put bookshelves in houses he built."

"Where did you get that bit of foolish information?" I asked. "Everyone knows that my husband built more bookshelves than any man in the world, certainly more than people were capable of filling with books and much less of reading. He was the most devout reader that ever lived. Our own libraries are enormous—more than you could dream to touch in your lifetime."

"I am glad to hear it," he said without gladness. "I love to read—that is all I do in my spare time. I like the paperbacks, don't you?"

"Yes," I answered, "but I also like beautifully bound books."

"I care for the content of a book," he said smugly, "not the way it looks."

"Why not have both—good content and good-looking binding?"

"My bank account won't permit it," he said. "The others are cheaper."

I could only wonder at this lean, pale man with long sharp-pointed mustache—the prominent president of a prominent museum in a prominent city—who could not afford well-bound books . . .

Later at coffee in the drawing room Mrs. John D. Rockefeller—aristocratic of bearing—graciously spoke to me of her admiration for Mr. Wright. Her aunt was Mrs. Avery Coonley for whom Mr. Wright had built a house in Riverside, Illinois, in 1908. Mr. Wright considered this to be his most successful house at that time and Mrs. Coonley his most enlightened client. Mrs. Rockefeller told me how happy her aunt was with her house.

Mary Moses, who originally came from Dodgeville, Wisconsin, cautioned me not to work too hard; not to do too much. Mary Moses is genuine—means what she says. Robert Moses is a lucky man to have her as his wife.

Driving up to the Museum for the second reception we saw elegantly-gowned women and tuxedoed men streaming through the glass doors. The great hall was filled with excitement when we entered to greet friends and to be introduced to more distinguished names.

Alicia moved with grace among her countless friends. On the second night of her duty as hostess her face was particularly delicate, almost transparent from the effect of the pleasurable ordeal. She kept introducing me swiftly and competently directing me to various clusters of her friends and acquaintances. She posed me for photographers. She moved on, greeting her own newspaper staff from *Newsday* with an ever lovely, fresh smile.

Accompanied by her husband, radiantly beautiful Helen Benton seemed to glow, enveloped in a silver gown to match her curly silver hair. I introduced her with pride to the Earl and the Countess Castle Stewart.

The Earl Castle Stewart told me in very English English how much he admired Mr. Wright. "In 1949 following Mr. Guggenheim's death, we held a meeting of the trustees in regard to the feasibility of building the Museum. Your husband was present and he handled the situation so admirably that we were all deeply impressed listening to him present his ideas in a clear, simple and direct way. When the meeting was concluded I walked over to him and congratulated him on the skill with which he had handled a group of experienced business men. Mr. Wright replied with a smile, 'It was just an expression of my belief that your father-in-law's dream will come true, my boy—that is all.'"

The Earl Castle Stewart, in his seventies, enjoyed the reference to him as "boy."

Familiar faces mingled with those of strangers looking about or gazing up in fascination at the great dome raised above their heads in peace and assurance. Space moved silently among the voices, lifting them along with its own motion, up toward the glass dome and on above the crashing noises of the machines in the city streets and still up—beyond the planes in the jammed sky.

On Wednesday, October twenty-first at noon, the third, final, formal and very official opening took place. We walked in with Maria and Edward Stone, who had picked us up at the Plaza in their car. The dignitaries, the press, the photographers and representatives of television, radio and "The Voice of America" filled the great hall and the ramps. Alicia introduced me to Bernard Baruch, Secretary Flemming and Mayor Wagner, after which I kept greeting my friends, and acquaintances from the previous occasions.

Robert Moses was at ease and at home, joking with the reporters and photographers. He appeared to know

186

them all. When the interviews were over we went in a procession into the beautiful auditorium-theater directly below the great hall. Though not asked to speak, I was conducted to a seat on the speakers' platform. What struck me was the peace that this circular auditorium conveyed, so gently did it hold us in its arms; so quiet, so perfect—untouched by human ignorance mistaken for "progress." It spoke its own silent language of beauty, divinity and immortality of the human soul. This hall was permeated with Mr. Wright's presence.

Men spoke, one after another. Harry Guggenheim, Robert Moses, Mayor Wagner, Henry Cabot Lodge, Secretary Flemming, the Countess Castle Stewart . . . They spoke well, with the ease of professional speakers. Harry Guggenheim showed particular skill in handling the introductions.

But the presence in the hall remained unperturbed by professional praise. And as we walked away the potent silence dissolved the voices into forgotten fragments of the past.

We formed another formal procession outside of the Museum where Mayor Wagner was to cut the white ribbon across the entrance, symbolizing the opening of the building to the public. A solid cluster of photographers and motion picture cameras faced directly in front of us. They were calling back and forth to Mayor Wagner. The Mayor—holding the scissors—was waiting for their signal to proceed. He started to cut, the photographers moved forward calling out again for

187

him to stop. Finally the scissors and the cameras clicked simultaneously. The ribbon was cut. A great mass of people stood on the street watching. The silence called to them to enter and partake of a world of beauty; a new vision into the future; a new promise for a better life.

Chapter 10

THE BETH SHOLOM SYNAGOGUE

A month earlier, on a bright crisp Sunday, I had gone to
Elkins Park, a suburb of Philadelphia, for the dedication of the Beth Sholom Synagogue which Mr. Wright
had designed in 1954. The congregation was seated
when I entered the Synagogue through the door next
to the pulpit. I was shown to my place in the first row.
Behind me were 1500 people. Twenty of our young
men and women from Taliesin filled the rows on the
right side. It was a glad sight for me.

The music of the organ rose to the pyramidal dome,
descended and hovered over us. Such great beauty
easily turns into pain. As the waves of sound kept rising
and falling, some faces glistened with tears.

It was not an easy thing to endure; not for those who,
as I, had seen the Synagogue being created on the
drafting boards, gradually developed and perfected by
Mr. Wright. They now saw the living, breathing or-
ganism in its breathtaking reality.

The religious procession which came from behind us
was most impressive: twelve men flanked by two on
either side carried Torahs wrapped in soft shades of
velvet with golden edging and placed them into the
Ark with solemn reverence.

189

The speeches were given in praise and remembrance of the work with Mr. Wright—the kindness, the receptiveness and the gentleness of his spirit. The choir and the deep longing voice of the cantor resounded in the building like an echo from Mount Sinai.

The dedication lasted for two and a half hours before my turn came to walk up the steps of the platform which Mr. Wright had designed, to the pulpit which he had designed with the seven-candled Menorahs standing on either side, and the soft light pouring down from the sky above my head.

Then I spoke to them, inspired as I was when I last sat in the Synagogue with him:

What can be greater than faith? Faith in man, in God and immortality of the human spirit? What can be greater than faith that is made manifest through man's thought, heart and action? What can be greater than a place in which he can momentarily withdraw himself from the chores and drudgeries of his physical existence to partake of meditation sacred to his spirit? And what can be greater than man's innermost fulfillment of an idea that he cherishes more highly than himself?

For thousands of years he has searched for it in loneliness and solitude.

He came near it in the glory of nature—in fields and meadows—in hills and mountains; he searched in the midst of multitudes where he yearned to feel himself a part of his world and his universe; and when life forced him to live in the city, he seldom experienced the desired union with God in the crowded streets and the crowded day of his work. So he built for himself temples of worship where he could withdraw within the realm of his inner world to be inspired and sustained by the expression of beauty that his temple might offer him.

And all of the millions of men on earth built themselves temples according to the tradition and heritage of their faith. And the truer the expression of man's heritage and his faith, the more perfect was the joy in which he exulted in union with his creator.

Among the oldest of religions is Judaism. This great ancient faith established the traditions, the laws, the ethical excellency of human conduct through the Torah, the Pentateuch, and sacred symbols. Eternal light and the seven-branched Menorah graced its temple. "And let them make me a sanctuary that I may dwell among them."

Judaism has flowed like a mighty river from generation to generation to extol man's deep communion with God, communion which was direct as man to man in its simple exposition of the profound significance of its faith.

The synagogue was the temple of worship of this ancient religion. But it never had an architectural expression of its own in the form appropriate to the principle of its faith. Through centuries of the alternating rise and fall of civilizations the temple underwent so many changes that its character, its power, and its inspiration were barely recognizable in architectural terms. The synagogue was subjected to many other influences: Assyrian, Babylonian and the Greek. The architectural character that the faith might have found for itself was completely lost as the ages replaced one another.

191

The twentieth century bore sterile impersonal architectural forms without the faintest semblance of the
principle which held above all the majestic sense that
man and God were one. Insignificant copies of copies
were scattered through the cities of the world. And the
synagogue stood humble on the street in ignorance of
its own inner power.

Then in this somber twentieth century of ours there
arose an architect—a man who daringly built a synagogue through which the voices of God and Moses were
called again to life in visible form. The spirit of Mount
Sinai grew on a street, independent, strong, declaring
its original faith when man spoke directly to God and
God answered man. Their voices ring through sheets
of glass and plastic, through steel and concrete, through
living forms of today, binding them with the power of
their noble past to seal their legacy to the Future. The
white light like the breath of God pours through the
walls and descends from the high pyramidal dome embracing the Torah, the eternal light; the Menorahs, the
voice of the cantor, the rabbi, and the throbbing silence
of the congregation.

Rare among men, this creator of new forms, when he
designed and built, gave to each great religious faith
its own symbol. This synagogue is the symbol of victory over the destructive forces and the persecution of
the Jewish faith. It is a new architectural expression
whose roots are dipped into the long measures of Time
—and which has once more risen in the proud dignity
and character of its faith. The temple fulfills the indestructible wish of the human soul to share in divine
beauty and to feel the presence of God.

192

Frank Lloyd Wright built the Synagogue on Old York Road in a section of a suburb called Elkins Park near the city called Philadelphia. Whoever comes to this Synagogue, to whatever faith he may belong, his heart will be purified and he will hear the voice of God in answer to his deep sorrow. For there is no one among us in this precarious age of nuclear menace that does not feel a deep sorrow within. There is no one among us who does not yearn for a higher force, divine in nature, to strengthen the love and understanding of his fellow man. This is our only weapon in the face of the newly risen enemy.

Many have already gone to the Beth Sholom Synagogue—the living symbol of Mount Sinai—as on a pilgrimage to refresh the spirit, to clarify the mind, and to purify the heart. And those whose heritage is the faith of Judaism will feel that once more they have come back home to their great religion to fortify their faith in man and God.

PART THREE

REMINISCENCES

The Wright-Jones family tree stretches out its long branches with many a leaflet attached to them. One such leaflet is Bitsy's son, Oliver, grandson of Maginel Wright Barney, who also came to the June 8th dinner.

Chubby-cheeked, with an upturned nose, a wholesome, typically American child, Oliver looked wistfully at our Lectracar-Surrey and said, "I wish I could ride in that."

"I'll give you a ride," I promised. But the care of many guests temporarily made me forget my promise. When his mother brought Oliver to me to say goodbye, I remembered. "Come with me," I said. "I'll give you the Surrey ride."

"Oh," Bitsy exclaimed, "how wonderful of you to do that! That's all he could talk about for the last 24 hours. He is dying to have a ride!"

Leaving all my guests behind, I put my arm around Oliver's shoulder but it seemed to me that my own steps were more eager than his when we walked to the upper court. He was looking down at something I could not see. We sat in the Surrey and off we went. But Oliver's eyelids were still lowered. "Look," I said, "isn't this wonderful? See the flowers, the trees . . . and if you wish, you can touch a branch as you go by."

"Uh huh," he said without looking. Then he added, "I think he is asleep now."

"Who is asleep?" I asked astonished.

"The moth, of course. Don't you see him? I caught him on the screen door of your house."

There on his tweed trousers clung a fragile little white moth. Oliver continued, "I think he is going to get a good rest now. And when he wakes up after getting his rest, I'm going to train him like a falcon. You know the kind of falcon you hold on your hand or on your shoulder and he stays there? You think that if I try hard I can train him like a falcon?" And the expression on his face was of tender love.

"I suppose you can," I sighed. "But, Oliver, look at the white swans on the lake—that is Jupiter and his handsome mate, Juno. After living many years alone, Jupiter found a mate he liked."

"Uh huh," he said, giving them a minute look and staring again at the moth. "I hope I can take him safely to New York. Do you think he'll enjoy flying to New York?"

"I'm sure he will," I sighed. "Do you like the hills, Oliver? See how beautiful they are covered with birches and fir trees."

"Uh huh," he said, flashing his look momentarily in their direction.

"How old are you, Oliver?" I asked.

"Ten," he said disinterestedly.

"You are just a little boy, aren't you?" I smiled at his round face and the short cropped hair.

I tried another tactic, "Oliver, you must not touch

the moth. They say that the dust comes off their wings when you touch them. You might have hurt him already —he may not be able to fly."

"Oh, no," he said. "Who told you that? Besides, I don't pet him on his wings. I pet his stomach. I caught him by the stomach, too."

I kept driving on the lovely Taliesin water-level road, smiling at the quaint little boy who had found a treasure.

He seemed a little worried, "I really didn't touch his wings. I didn't hurt him. Look!" And he picked up the moth beneath his wings and deftly stroked his body which he called the stomach.

I stopped by a field of tall grass which waved in plastic motion. "Oliver," I said, "look at the way the wind moves the grass."

He actually raised his blue eyes and said, "How very pretty. I like that big tree. It is such a pretty tree." And for a few moments I had won over his fascination with the moth. Then he said, "I am glad he is taking such a long nap—he won't be tired for the trip then."

"I'm sure he won't," I answered. By this time I had given up.

When we drove up to the Taliesin court, his mother was waiting for us.

"Oliver, wasn't that nice of Aunt Olgivanna to have given you your ride?"

"Uh huh," he said, looking at the moth.

Then his mother, smartly dressed to leave for the big city, said with a child-like shimmer in her eyes, "Please, will you give me just a short ride around the court?"

"I will take you all the way down to the lake," I

said. And we noiselessly pulled away in the little yellow Surrey. Our niece, Bitsy, her hair swept back by the wind, bubbling with delight and joy, drew deep breaths of sun-soaked air, filled with the wonder of the shrubs, flowers and bowing grass. She could not take her eyes off the colorful treasures which nature gave us that morning, as her son Oliver could not take his eyes off the mysterious white moth—the sleeping beauty caught in his hand.

Bitsy, Elizabeth Enright Gillham, the daughter of Maginel Barney, is the distinguished writer of stories and of children's books. Collections of her stories, many of which have appeared in the *New Yorker* and other leading magazines, have been published under the titles *Borrowed Summer, The Moment Before the Rain,* and *The Riddle of the Fly.* Some of her tales are so potent and her power of observation so cutting that I told her, "At times you leave me robbed of everything; in my hands a sun-dried bone; in my soul a sense of doom." She was pleased.

But to look at our elegant niece no one would guess this quality of her talent. She has laughing blue-grey eyes, a perky nose, and a softly rounded face. Golden cherub-like hair curls about her pretty head. The movements of her body are swift and spirited.

Her relationship with her famous uncle was gay and filled with humor. He called her lovingly "Bitsy-Ritzy of New York." She in turn liked to tease him. She tells how her uncle at a cocktail party, meeting an old friend, affectionately patted the man on his well-rounded proof of good living, "Who fashioned this for you?"

"An Architect greater than you," retorted the quick-witted friend.

"And the only greater one," Mr. Wright threw back over his shoulder.

Some twenty-five years ago, Bitsy spent the summer at Taliesin. One afternoon she and I drove to Dodge-ville to do some shopping where I bought a quaint apron with a pattern of green flowers. When I put it on, I noticed that a small, crooked green pocket was stitched to the apron so low that my hand could barely reach into it. She teased me about this but I insisted that the apron was pretty just the same and when we returned to Taliesin, I immediately ripped the pocket off and threw it into a waste paper basket. We lunched together and when I came back to my room the pocket was pinned with a flower to my mirror. I crumpled it smiling and threw it out again. The next day I put the apron on to find the pocket sewn back into the same place! Once more I took it off but this time, wrapping it carefully in many layers of tissue paper, I placed it in a large box. I then tied the package with a yellow ribbon and asked one of our boys to present her with this gift from me. After disposing of the endless wrappings she finally saw the green pocket lying mockingly on a cushion of red satin. Bitsy exclaimed, "I will get even with her for this!"

From then on the green pocket was woven as a gay pattern into our relationship. Sometimes she or I would keep it as long as two or three years until both of us had forgotten about it. Then the green pocket would appear again in all its frayed but insolent defiance.

When we were in New York many years ago, Bitsy brought me a gardenia and pinned it on my dress with a bewitching smile, which only later did I realize was the smile of a Benedict Arnold. To her fiendish delight I wore the gardenia all evening without noticing a thing. When I returned to the hotel and took it off I watched in helpless rage the wrinkled pocket sliding down the stem. And as I raged on, Mr. Wright laughed, "She put it over on you, didn't she?"

Then once I brought her a Cracker Jack box from Spring Green. "How did you know that I love Cracker Jacks?" she asked pleased and, suspecting nothing, opened the box. Among the surprises was the green pocket. She hurled it on the table and screamed, "I will never forgive you for this! I forgot all about the hideous thing."

The ingenuity that went into disguising this object from year to year became increasingly subtle. Our imaginative, dashing, wicked niece presented me with a lovely 1840 cut-out English Victorian collage print— framed under glass. "Oh, thank you," I said appreciatively. "I have always wanted to own one of these! Look," I showed it proudly to Mr. Wright, "isn't this a delicate color scheme?" and I, myself, examined it more closely. . . . And while she stood there curling a treacherous lip, I suddenly saw that the pocket though diabolically concealed was glittering with gold on the green skirt of the duchess.

This was too much. In desperation I poured green

plastic over the pocket, molded it into an ash tray and sent it to her. This handiwork of mine stalled the exchange for quite some time. To my smug satisfaction I heard later from her mother the trouble she had in retrieving the pocket.

Many hard experiences took place in the following lean years of our relationship. We barely saw one another—she was deep in writing and lecturing and I preoccupied in my own complex life. The lines of our destiny went in opposite directions.

Then, in 1957, I received a package from Bitsy. It was a green silk evening dress with long sleeves. The Christmas card attached had the old English poem "Green Sleeves"—but it conveyed nothing to me. I wore the dress on many occasions and then one evening at dinner I felt something rip on the inside of the left cuff. As I pulled at the loose piece of cloth I drew out the pocket! I gave a little cry but caught myself in time—our guests had turned to me in surprise. I quickly slipped it in my evening bag and continued discussing art and politics. Up to that moment the pocket had been extinguished in my memory. Oh, to have fallen into such a masterly and well-timed trap set by my incomparable adversary!

The pocket had been in my possession for two years when we again met at the Plaza in New York. Bitsy looked very chic, the epitome of elegance, wearing a striking green necklace for which I expressed my enthusiasm profusely as a new scheme developed in my mind. A Valentine for Bitsy! When I returned to Arizona I bought a black straw hat in Scottsdale and trimmed it with red cherries and green leaves. I cut red felt in the shape of a heart, and placed it on the upper part of the brim. Over it I arranged in a semi-circle five small hearts made in several layers of red, green, yellow, orange, turquoise and black felt. In the third layer of the second appliquéd heart, lies unobtrusively and neatly tucked in, the green pocket.

The hat has style. It must look beautiful on glamorous Bitsy. With what pleasure she must innocently be wearing it on her lovely golden curls.

But, of course, you realize this must remain entirely between you and me.

A great many new interests have evolved in my life due to our son-in-law, Wesley Peters, and our grandson, Brandoch, about which I never would have otherwise known. It is not at all peculiar, for instance, to find myself a frequent visitor of aviaries, zoological gardens and pet shops of all kinds.

Brandoch invited me once to go to the Phoenix Bird-Park. While there I had the uneasy feeling of being followed everywhere by two huge Australian emus that resemble ostriches. Their peculiar naked eyes never left sight of mine; but it was particularly unpleasant that their eyes were on the level of my own. Brandoch assured me that they liked me and that was why they were so closely following me. I did at one point cling to him for protection because the profile of one of those sloppily-feathered birds was just a few inches away from mine.

Unwisely, I mentioned how nice it would have been

to have a crane walking beside me instead. At that instant Brandoch showed me two striking black and gold African cranes who wore golden crowns on their heads. Brandoch eagerly urged me to get one of them and all that afternoon I had to protect myself from getting involved in buying a crane. "I have enough to do without a crane added," I complained. "I don't want to look after a crane. My dog, Casanova, is enough."

Passing by a large cage we saw a black sleek mynah bird who introduced himself without inhibition: "My name is Charlie. What is yours?" Fortunately for me Brandoch already had a talking mynah bird whose name is Oscar and I did maneuver leaving without the brash Charlie. Brandoch then tempted me with two soft pink cockatoos. Although every time we approached them they purred a tender, demure, appealing "hello"—I bravely resisted Brandoch's and their captivating charms.

We tore ourselves away from the cages and went back to the car where Casanova was waiting, screaming —tortured and frustrated by the close presence and delightful odors of the birds.

Eagles are the bane of my life. No sooner does one of those cruel birds get loose and fly away than Wes and Brandoch get another. The last one was a huge eagle from Montana. And all of our Taliesin mothers were afraid for the safety of their children. Said they: "That awful new eagle has talons as large as a man's fist!" At which Wes sneered, "Most ridiculous hysteria. The bird is as docile as a dove!" But everyone was greatly relieved when this eagle also disappeared into the mountains.

When in New York I often visit museums or explore

the antique shops that line Third Avenue. To the surprise of store owners I ask to see old Japanese, Persian, Chinese and Tibetan swords; suits of armor and coats of mail; daggers and old rifles; and falcons and eagles made of iron or brass that ornamented medieval fireplaces.

I know quite well the period of the Middle Ages to which Wes might have so naturally belonged. His is the domain of the feudal baron, feasting in great halls lighted by torches, the long oaken tables arrayed with golden goblets and hounds lying on bearskins at his feet. He likes massive rings worn by the lords of those ages, and seals of various past centuries.

How many times I have sat in some wobbly old chair to rest in a dusty antique shop, amid swords, daggers and old pistols . . . feeling uncertain in making a choice in this strange and purely masculine world.

I am now entering an entirely new field—ancient coins. I am learning about the coins of Albania, Greece, and the Roman and Byzantine Empires. Wes was extremely excited the other day while showing me a peculiar coin. "This is the 'Widow's Mite' of the New Testament story," he said enthusiastically. It was a tiny little piece made of blackened bronze that looked fearfully worn and old. "And this coin might have been the very one Jesus held in His hand when He said, 'Render therefore unto Caesar the things which are Caesar's,' " he added exultingly. And, of course, it might have been.

The coins are beautiful bas-relief engravings of emperors of the past. My knowledge being quite new, I have not yet acquired the eye of the connoisseur. I have to be told which profile belongs to which emperor and the time of his reign. But I am learning.

Wes is also interested in Indian blankets and old silver and leather concho belts. He is thoroughly acquainted with Indian folklore and knows all the tribes. He often displays to some friend the Navajo chief warrior blanket, wrapping it around himself while relating at length the whole history of the tribe to whom the blanket belonged.

And, of course, it is of the utmost importance to him that people show interest in his interests.

He is an avid chess player. I have spent many a Christmas season looking for unusual chess sets for him. But on one thing I have stood my ground in spite of all his and Brandoch's cunning schemes to teach me— I have flatly refused to learn to play chess. He has taught many of our friends and apprentices, but still I have stood firm on my ground. No chess! Every now and then he organizes tournaments at Taliesin. Large groups divide into pairs and suddenly sink into silence. They sit wordless on the sun-terrace, in the apprentice courts, at the swimming pool, bending down with faces that exclude all life around them.

He and Brandoch often played this tedious brain-exhausting game with self-consuming attention while Mr. Wright and I contented ourselves with a simple game of checkers. "I concentrate all day long on my work," Mr. Wright said. "Why should I add another burden to my concentration? I don't need to work my brain that way."

Wes took this jibe with royal bearing. "Too bad. You are missing so much fun by not playing this most noble of games," he would say with lordly compassion.

Among Wes' best friends at Taliesin West is my brother Vlado, who also belongs to Taliesin's inner circle of chess nobility. Vlado, the idol of my childhood and youth, and his gentle Sophie have stayed with us in the desert for the last fifteen years. They watch over the camp through the year and like especially their summer solitude in the desert. Both of them had a deep love for Mr. Wright and understanding of his architecture. Mr. Wright was fond of them in turn.

"Vlado has a fine mind," Mr. Wright said, "and knows more about politics than some of our prominent politicians do". . . and about Sophie: "Her love of Vlado is that of a saint. That is one of her most admirable qualities. I am glad we have them with us."

And how grateful I am. Since April ninth we have sat together many a time and their presence has made the irreparable loss somewhat easier to bear.

Brandoch breezed into my room late one night—"I just got in—drove the Dusenberg down from L. A.," he said with exhilaration.

"What?" I asked. "Did the old battleship actually make it?"

"Gana, wait till you see it. It is the swellest car on the road. I drove steadily at sixty miles an hour with not one bit of trouble. I will take you for a ride tomorrow."

"Oh," I groaned, "must I go through that again? The last time you gave me a ride in your Dusenberg, the radiator burst, the cap flew off, a geyser of hot water shot in the air and almost scalded us."

"But, Gana, you don't understand. It has been fixed since; it is practically a new car now."

"Oh, I know but I won't go this time. You and your daddy enjoy your rides. Please don't ask me."

In the morning we went to the parking lot and there was the twenty-five-year-old Dusenberg looking dignified in classic style. I could not believe my eyes. The car, completely overhauled, painted some fifty coats of Chinese Lacquer Red, with a tan top and brown leather upholstery, refinished chromium, had elegant simplicity and flawless lines. This was a change! Wes opened the car's hood and showed me the engine in all its streamlined perfection.

"This engine was the first in the world to have dual overhead camshafts," he said with gluttonous joy. "This is a model F Riviera. A Dusenberg model F in good condition should be able to go from zero to a hundred miles an hour in twenty-two seconds! That was in 1934. There were only six of this particular model made.

"They no longer make automobiles of such incredible workmanship and excellent materials. The car originally cost $15,000 during the depression. Each was individually hand-built by the Dusenberg brothers. Not one car was like any other. Each car was improved over the one they had just finished."

Of course I did not ask how much he had invested in it in the last few years, but he certainly had brought the car up to date in every way.

Later that morning Wes, Brandoch and I called on the William Bentons and their children John and

Louise. We displayed the car to them from every angle.
To the happy satisfaction of Wes and Brandoch, Mr.
Benton thought that the Dusenberg was a new foreign
car! That, I told them, was the peak they had never
dreamt of reaching.

"Oh no, Gana, the greatest peak we have reached
was getting you in the car and liking it!" Brandoch said
appreciatively.

Then we drove to Celia Peabody's house; she came
out to admire the car, but she was more blasé than
the Benton family.

"I owned several Dusenbergs in the past," she said
casually. "This is an awfully good job you have done,
Wes. The car looks fine."

Celia invited us to come in. Her elegant, well-kept
house stands high on the side of Camelback Mountain.
Her monkeys still occupied their usual seats. Celia likes
monkeys. She has eighty-five of them in all sizes and
varieties. The largest one is about three feet high, the
smallest about an inch and a half. Fortunately they are
of cloth, wood and porcelain. Her friends, knowing her
unique passion for monkeys, give them to her as gifts.

I personally do not quite enjoy having such a multitude of monkeys with their sad mute eyes watching me
from chairs, tables, beds, shelves, bureaus, and desks
—but they do perhaps inspire gratitude in recognition
of the fact that "there but for the grace of God go I."

Over the fireplace in her large living room hangs a
stuffed sailfish which stretches the full length of seven
feet, gleaming in silver and sailing full sail across the
room.

"I caught that fish in Acapulco. I pulled him in myself!" Celia said with pride. "It was not an easy job, but I made it—the fish weighed 760 pounds!" Although it is an unusual decoration for a lady's parlor, I have to admit it is picturesque and gives the room a dashing air.

My sophisticated and warm-hearted friend once told me, "I worshipped my father. While he was still a young student at Yale his father died, leaving him ten million dollars. Of course ten million dollars was a lot of money in those days—it is nothing now. . . ." I smiled. So innocently sincere she was! "And my father," she continued, "divided his own share among his six sisters. He was a wonderful man."

Tall Celia looked stunning in her lounging pajamas of exotic, shimmering satins and silks. "I love to wear my old riding outfit, battered hat, comfortable boots," she said, inhaling a deep puff of her cigarette. "I went to Vi McNeil's ranch the other day—she needed help in rounding up her steers. Near the end of the roundup while she was being assisted by several of her cowboys in branding the animals, my eye caught a large lazy calf dreamily munching hay. I decided to try my luck, and while Vi was not looking, I rushed to the calf, threw him on the ground and hog-tied him! Vi screamed, not believing what she saw. I thought, myself, that I did pretty well!"

Celia is also handy with a shotgun and she is a splendid horsewoman. "I rode horseback from Nogales, Mexico, to Tucson, about sixty miles distance," she said. "We went on pack horses, which took us four days. What a wonderful experience that was! I just love the outdoor life."

My paradoxical friend is thoughtful and sensitive.
Her blue eyes turn deep cornflower purple when filled
with tears. She willingly takes upon herself a share of
sorrow to lighten the hearts of those who suffer.

Kay came to study architecture at Taliesin at the age
of sixteen and eventually became my secretary. She is
frail and slight, about five feet tall, yet if one of our
boys would hesitate in turning a big table around, she
would plunge forward and deftly move the table into
exact position.

When Kay painted portraits, she always made the
subject in the picture look the way she liked him to
look; when she painted landscapes she planted trees,
flowers, fields and grass wherever she pleased. When
she said, for instance, "I have just painted Joe," no one
paid any attention—no one recognized Joe, and everyone raved about the portrait! If she pointed out to some
naïve apprentice the location of the landscape she had
just painted, he blinked several times, looking back and
forth at the canvas, then blushed and mumbled, "It
resembles it a lot," and disappeared. Kay would smile
and say, "What a funny boy."

If my Weimaraner, Casanova, snatched a piece of
candy, she would open his mouth and, forcing her little
hand in, pull the candy out from all the way down his
throat—Kay was always just one second faster than he.
Casanova would give her a look of awe and hate. This
"fight" was quite regular. He would sometimes grab a

piece of candy right out of her hand, looking at her challengingly, and try fiercely to flip his tongue fast to get it down—but Kay would make one streaking dash, her hand was down his throat and poor Casanova always lost!

Snakes and Kay also challenged one another. Many years ago she and I went far into the desert to paint. It was the middle of May and very hot. We were in sunsuits and wore sandals on our bare feet. I was concentrating deeply on my painting while she, as usual, having finished her sketch first, was standing a few feet away from me. "Do you know what I am looking at?" she asked in a dreamy tone of voice.

"No," I answered vaguely.

"I am looking down at a very pretty coral snake."

I raised my eyes. Kay's foot was a few inches from the snake! They were looking straight at one another. "Step quickly away," I whispered horrified. "That is one of the most poisonous snakes. Are you out of your mind?"

But before she did so, the snake slid on its coral way into the desert! Kay triumphed over all difficulties in this most casual way.

She kept the list of work rotation for the apprentices so that I could direct it from week to week. She did this work entirely in her own peculiar way. If, for instance, I asked her what work John had been doing in the last several months outside of his drafting room assignment, she would simply look at her chart and tell me with immediate precision, "He was on sanitation, on theater decoration, on dining room" and so on.

"Let me see your chart," I would ask. It was filled

with a variety of hieroglyphics purely of her own invention, each symbol denoting the type of work. Thus she saved both labor and space.

If she went on a trip, whoever took over this book of hers wrung his hands and became frantic trying to decipher her enigmatic code. And if someone was bold enough to substitute words for symbols, she was outraged and put her own "system" back into order. She is Swiss.

Kay took care of my bills also in her own fashion. Once I received a letter from a bookstore, whose owner I know personally, expressing surprise at my not having taken care of a bill. I, too, was surprised and called Kay in.

"Oh, I wanted to teach them a lesson," she said. "When I asked them to send the books collect, they should have done so. It was just careless of them to do a thing like that!"

"Please, Kay—don't teach business people their business, but pay the bills as they come!"

"But, Mrs. Wright, they were wrong," she insisted. "I wrote to them already that they had upset my accounts."

"What is the use?" I said, and gave up.

Kay could cook a perfect meal at any time and in the shortest time of anyone in the Fellowship. Those little fingers of hers went through beans, peas, lettuce, onions, radishes with a dazzling speed. She rocked the huge frying pan containing French fried potatoes as though it were made of tin instead of iron. Large ladles and spatulas were swung around and everyone and everything in sight was sizzling. She could straighten out kitchen emergencies in a few seconds and she could reason anyone, including herself, in and out of everything. Dick Carney was once found lying down in the library flat on his back and desperate. "You know what Kay said to me?" he groaned. "She said that I might have killed Mr. and Mrs. Wright because I did not boil the string beans twenty minutes!"

But through all this Kay appeared on our Saturday and Sunday evenings glittering with rhinestones and sweet smiles as though she had been forgiven by everyone for everything. "Kay is the best clothes horse we have—this stubborn young Swiss," Mr. Wright used to say with a gentle smile.

When her father, Heinrich Schneider, a well known mechanical engineer and inventor, brought Kay to Taliesin he said, "Mrs. Wright, she is so little. Please take care of her." But anyone who tried to take care of Kay found himself taken care of instead.

On one of his visits her father remarked thoughtfully in his strong Swiss accent, "Kay chose the wisest life of them all, I am glad she is here with you—it gives me peace."

Tal Davison, the sixteen-year-old son of Kay and Davy, was sent by his paternal grandmother to a private school in the East. He had been attending the public school in Scottsdale, Arizona at the time, which he fully enjoyed. But feeling gratitude for his grandmother's generosity, he graciously accepted the change and flew East into a new life. Tal had never gone to a private school before and his grandmother wanted him to get some of the good "polish" that such a school might give.

After a few days there, he telephoned me feeling rather sad, but I reminded him, "You have a change of conditions now; it is what you wanted. You have been telling me that one should see something other than Taliesin. You were born and have lived here all your life, you said, and you wanted to see the world. Here is a chance for you to meet an entirely different set of young people. I should think that would be very good."

"O.K." he said, and his voice had a sense of futility about any kind of reaction after my powerful reminder.

Then he wrote to me:

"Dear Mrs. Wright,

"This school bores me. Every day the same routine. We have chapel once a day and sometimes twice. We bow down to the sixth form and masters. I do think this is good for me somewhat, but there is hardly any freedom.

"There is a dance occasionally, but the masters don't let you out of their sight.

"The education will do me good in the future, but I hope this school does not influence me. I don't want to be called 'too cultivated'; but I do want good intellect. Actually I think it is stupid to close someone up like this just for education. Really, I want to bust out sometimes!

"This is one of the first real changes in my life. There is nothing to look forward to. I like a little freedom. There is none here. I have never been so un-independent in my whole life!

"I really liked what I had at Taliesin.

"I know I didn't work at my studies, but I am older now.

"Private school gives a good education, but I don't think it is worth the sacrifices. The only way to get along in this school is to *be* boring!

"In Wisconsin this summer I was anxious, as you might know, to get back to Arizona. I have many good and interesting friends of both sexes which I miss.

"I will miss you and everyone at Taliesin. I think I made a very foolish decision coming here. But, of course, I did think I would like it. But it is so dead! You once said it was bad not to have any freedom. Well, there is none here.

"But I made a mistake and I will have to suffer, I guess. I know this sounds real sad, but what can I do? And I don't want to hurt my grandmother.

"I was wondering how my parents felt about it. You see with Celeste away, and Daddy's back trouble.

"I am sort of mixed up and really don't know what to do. Please, let me know what you think. If I was to leave, it wouldn't be hard to start school in Arizona. The work is just about the same.

Love,
Tal"

He called me later. "Mrs. Wright, did you get my letter?"

"Yes, Tal—I did," I answered. "But a little discipline like that ought to be good for you. You may have had too much freedom in your life."

"That isn't it, Mrs. Wright. It is just so dead here," he repeated. "You don't know. *You* couldn't stand it!"

"Well, I probably couldn't right now, Tal. But I don't think it is fair to your grandmother. She has paid $2,500 for you. How can we do a thing like that to her?"

"I have a good idea. I have already talked it over with the headmaster," Tal answered enthusiastically. "My tuition from this private school can be transferred to the Judson private school in Paradise Valley near Taliesin West. I could become a day pupil there, and it will cost just half of the tuition here which they said they will return, so grandmother won't lose anything. I could then have some normal freedom and still be in a private school."

"I see," I said, "you are killing two birds with one stone! I have no objection. Go ahead and put it through with your grandmother. That way you won't hurt her feelings and perhaps you will still have more severe discipline there than in the public school."

"Oh, Mrs. Wright," he said happily. "Now may I talk with my father?"

The result of it was that Tal managed the whole business end of it with such skill that he might well have been schooled in the business world all his life! He flew to Taliesin West, joined the Judson School and with his grandmother's blessings.

Tal proved to be well equipped for life, yet he obviously showed himself to be a non-conformist. He did not want to accept a routine in which he did not believe, and he knew how to deal with a complex situation. A less independent boy most probably would have succumbed, believing the problem insoluble.

Tal had a sense of honor. Doubtless he lay awake nights thinking his way out of a desperate plight so as not to hurt anyone. As a result his grandmother was happy because she was doing something for him that both she and he believed in; his father and mother were happy because they had their son with them; and we were happy because Tal showed the right spirit of rebellion.

John deKoven Hill joined the Taliesin Fellowship when he was still in his teens, a rather reticent and shy boy just out of high school in Evanston, Illinois. He stayed sixteen years, from 1938 to 1953, participating in the hard work and acquiring the discipline that Taliesin training gives. He worked in the fields and in the kitchen; he learned to draw, to do carpentry, masonry, gardening and interior decorating. I believe that John has helped me redecorate every room at Taliesin, Tan-y-deri and Midway in Wisconsin, and at Taliesin West in Arizona.

"John is unusually artistic," Mr. Wright often said. "This boy will do good work some day." And John Hill has done a remarkably fine piece of work that Mr. Wright would have been proud of. The February 1960 issue of *House Beautiful* Magazine was devoted entirely to a house designed and built by John Hill and chosen by *House Beautiful as* "the pace setter of 1960." This work bears the mark of a noble influence, and the inspiration he has drawn from this noble source should last him his lifetime.

His house, built of Indiana limestone concrete, wood and metal, lies on the green with comfort and ease, embracing the hill with natural grace.

It overlooks the Ohio River. The materials are used

with understanding and love—and that is what marks this house as a work of art.

Every rock, every board, every detail was handled by John Hill with the tenderness of an artist. Not only has he a feeling for texture, but he has that rare gift, a sense of proportion. As a true artist he knows exactly when to stop in his freely evolving forms—one of the most difficult things to achieve in any creative field. He handles his work with strong judgment, allowing nothing to minimize the practical side of the dwelling and yet not sacrificing one aspect of the beauty which radiates throughout the whole structure.

Even in the service court and laundry drying yard, screened by graceful aluminum tracery, John Hill makes a beautiful circumstance out of a work place, using the screen to provide free air circulation for drying the laundry.

Similar perforated, patterned, anodized aluminum grilles of soft blue-green add an ethereal delicacy to the enclosed space throughout the house. They are used along the upper living room clerestories in long rectangular panels which give a sense of transparency, a floating quality to the ceiling of silky wood. This poetic, airy lightness is contrasted with strong stone piers and the massive fireplace. By such interplay of strength and delicacy, John Hill has created a richly varied atmosphere. We never tire of work which evokes in us a creative reaction, an impulse toward beauty.

John Hill is Editorial Director of *House Beautiful*, one of the most influential magazines of its kind in America, and has also been a designer of buildings and furniture, and a lecturer.

After he left Taliesin he kept in uninterrupted contact with us. There is a family relationship of spirit that unites us, as with the majority of our students who stay at Taliesin for several years. Wherever they happen to be in the world, we hear from them about their experiences.

While he was in Japan on a magazine assignment recently, I received a letter from John. His keen visual perception of the minutest details is as extraordinary as his appreciation of beauty and grace.

"Kyoto, Japan.—It is so easy to see why Mr. Wright loved this country so much. The people are all sweet, natural, and in spite of western clothes and building there is a special charm everywhere. The only strain is the language barrier. Even when they speak English I can't understand them! Everywhere I'm introduced with long speeches, with 'Wright-san' inserted often and 'Keehahoo Hoteru,' which seems to be Imperial Hotel . . . We've been staying in Japanese inns—beautiful rooms with matting and no furniture but always flowers, paintings, beautiful dishes and lacquer . . . We go to Tokyo about the eighteenth and stay at the Imperial. It will probably seem pretty good to get up off the floor . . . When the sun is out it's glorious but sleeping on the floor when it's cold and rainy is really chilling even with a two-ton quilt!

". . . I'm sitting on a *zabotan,* a flat pillow on the floor, the shutters and sliding doors are open. There is a tiny enclosed garden with a cherry and a maple tree, some carefully shaped small bushes, a little stone water basin, and a lantern. The ground is covered with lush green moss. The room has a low square red lacquer table in the center, a good *kakimono* and a flower arrangement . . . I keep writing about all these little things because the overall impact is so great I can't put it into words. . . ."

I am glad that John Hill went to Japan. I know that the Japanese people will have one more opening through which to see into the life of true Americans. Because wherever John Hill will go, he will carry with him the gentleness of his spirit which will be conveyed to the people he meets. We need every possible means to establish friendly relations with other countries, and his will be an added contribution toward that end. Under the present explosive conditions in the world, the more understanding we gain of others the farther away will be the dread of war, and so we may eventually win the long struggle for a permanent peace.

Richard E. Carney is the son of a Baptist minister. He was in the last world war prior to joining the Taliesin Fellowship in 1948. Private Carney was sent abroad and his battalion was among the very first to counterattack the Germans in the Battle of the Bulge. With shells flying low and near, Dick Carney was in foxholes holding his own with the rest of the men.

Early on Christmas morning, dreary and grey, he and his companions were crouching in the cold, thinking of their distant land, expecting the Germans to attack any minute. "I had no hope for myself," said Dick. "I really cared for nothing. Sore in every limb, I could hardly hang on to my rifle when I saw a sergeant coming toward us calling out, 'Private Carney, Private Carney.' I reported to him. He handed me a telegram saying, 'This is from Eisenhower.' I could not believe what I read: 'To the Commanding Officer, 36th Armd Inf Reg., thru channels. 1. Private First Class Richard E. Carney has a principle appointment from the First Congressional District of Missouri to the United States Military Academy at West Point. 2. He is to be immediately removed to a safe area for possible return to continental United States pending results of physical examination. Signed, Eisenhower, Commanding General, Allied Expeditionary Forces.'"

Dick, dazed and as though moving in a dream, bade farewell to his comrades. He marched away with the sergeant, his hand on the breast pocket where the telegram lay. He was taken to the regimental adjutant who told him to look for a hospital and get a physical examination. Dick put his rifle on his shoulder and headed for the road, thinking of his father's sermons on miracles and praying for his comrades in the foxholes. He walked and hitch-hiked until he reached the first medical station.

Everyone was busy with the wounded. They had neither time nor equipment to give him the required tests. Dick understood only too well and, feeling guilty for taking the physician's time, he was glad when the doctor-in-chief directed him to a larger medical station. Again he walked and hitch-hiked for miles to another medical post. There he dropped exhausted and fell asleep on the steps of the hospital.

Dick woke up to see the ambulances driving up and

the wounded being carried in one after another. Waiting for hours for an appointment with the doctor, he was told in the end that they had no time to spend on him; there were thirty-six operations to be performed that day! The doctors told him to look for a larger medical center.

In the meantime during his quest for a hospital he was stopped off and on by American M.P.'s looking for German spies dressed in American uniforms who, it was rumored, were being dropped behind our lines for espionage work. Every time Dick was stopped, with a trembling hand he took out of his pocket the yellow faded telegram from the General of the Army with which he was allowed to proceed on his way.

Dick's journey on foot and by chance rides continued until he reached the city of Liege. There at long last he found a large hospital and finally received his examination. This time they had to accept him because that was the highest medical echelon. He was given every conceivable test. The X-rays were countless. His tests were all-inclusive, in accordance with the West Point admission standards. The report from the hospital was sent to Washington through channels—that is, it had to go through the chain of officials from lower to higher ranks in order to be examined by each until it reached the Surgeon General's office. So Dick Carney had to wait for the reply from Washington. He reported to his regimental adjutant, who tried to assign him to various sections of the division's rear. But knowing his status each group refused to accept him—they did not want the responsibility for his safety. Finally the Personnel Office was ordered to take him since that was the safest group in the Division!

However, the regiment belonged to one of the fastest armored divisions, named Spearhead. "We were constantly on the move," Dick reminisced, "because we had to keep within a certain distance of the front line of our Spearhead. That meant that our entire division was ahead of everyone else's front lines. We went so fast through the German towns that we had no time to take over the administration of the towns. So the German officials were left in charge after they surrendered. Almost daily we set up an office in a new town. When once I asked a German mayor of the town for office quarters, he replied, 'When we occupied Paris, we were polite to the French. If you are polite, no harm will befall you.'" The furthest thing from Dick's mind was to be impolite!

But the villagers were not so friendly. "I read in Paracelsus," Dick said, "that the victors entering a conquered country feel the negative vibrations of all they caused to die. These influences are so powerful that the suicide rate among the victors becomes alarming. This thought went through my mind as we pushed deeper into devastated Germany."

Having been assigned to a non-commissioned officer to be his assistant, Dick helped him make out the payroll for the regiment, sometimes amounting to almost a million dollars. However, the currency being Belgian, neither to Dick nor the other soldiers did it look like or even mean—money. So it was handled by all without due appreciation.

The war ended.

Within a month the non-commissioned officer for whom Dick worked was eligible and went home. Dick was now the only one who, more or less, knew how to run the office. So, at the age of twenty, he was promoted from Private First Class to Technical Sergeant and was placed in charge of the entire office with the title of Personnel Sergeant Major. This was an unheard of promotion under ordinary circumstances.

Dick ran the office as best he knew how. The responsibilities were to maintain complete records of each soldier in the regiment amounting to 1,500 men. The postwar army all over Europe was constantly being re-organized. Throughout a three month period, Dick Carney and his office of fifty assistants handled the records of five thousand men.

Swamped with such work, Dick forgot about his pending West Point appointment. One day he received a letter from Washington. Then he remembered. The letter informed him that due to the extreme irregularity of his teeth he could not be admitted to West Point.

Betty Cass was among our early friends in Madison. At the time Mr. Wright and I first knew her, she was a columnist on the *Wisconsin State Journal* in Madison. Betty frequently visited Taliesin in those years, picking up what material she could find for her column and always contributing to our social life.

Pretty and fair of complexion, with blue eyes and light brown hair, she appeared gay and quite carefree. It was not until later that I discovered the underlying tragedy of her life. None of it was expressed in either her actions or in the care of her four children with whom she was happy and companionable. Her daughter, Alice, was the same age as our daughter, Iovanna.

The two girls became close friends and thus was sealed the relationship between Betty and me. It was then I learned that Alice had a congenital and incurable defect of the heart and the doctors informed the mother that her little girl had a very short future.

Betty Cass kept writing humorous, witty columns, took additional editing jobs on magazines, working hard to support her children. She betrayed none of the pain while being fully aware of the inevitable.

Alice and Iovanna played well together but as their years moved from twelve to thirteen to fourteen, red-haired, sweet-faced Alice began to fade. She visited us with her mother at Taliesin West. We had many distinguished guests that Sunday night; among them the Metropolitan Opera star Lucrezia Bori. I told her of Alice and of her dream to be an opera singer. . . . Miss Bori was very kind to her.

Soon after, the blow struck little Alice. I shall never forget when I walked into Betty's apartment. She was sitting erect in a chair, clad in a navy blue tailored bathrobe, looking very neat, as usual. But very small and frail. Her blue eyes were full of tears, and she smiled.

The years went on. They must have been a new kind of years for her. She worked still harder to maintain her family.

Then the blow struck at Taliesin. Our older daughter Svetlana was gone. Betty Cass walked beside me on the road. "This is the worst thing that can happen to you," she kept repeating to me. "It will be a little better later. There will be some terrible days for years. Remember, however, this is the worst thing that can happen to you."

My friend spoke from *her* experience. But life can hold more than one deadly arrow.

In the last years I have had little contact with her except on June 8th, Mr. Wright's birthday. Her three boys have since grown and married, yet Betty always has remained young, always appearing neat and smartly dressed. She lived her life alone.

When I started writing columns for the *Capital Times,* the most appreciative of my critics was Betty Cass. Whenever she read a column that particularly moved her to thought, to tears or to laughter, she wrote me an enthusiastic letter. I especially appreciated her reaction because a columnist of some twenty years is apt to be professionally critical of one who has only recently embarked on that same field. But sorrow dug deep into the heart has its own way of gradually replacing standard values with higher ones.

After Nikita Khrushchev left the United States we seemed to have less "entertainment" as we read the newspapers or turned on the radio or television. The stocky, stout, round-faced man became a familiar figure to the citizens of the United States in 1959. His gentle, sweet-looking wife roly-polying along the streets also became known to us all.

What was accomplished by these two great countries on both sides? It is not only the governments that have been affected by the visit—it is all the people of the United States and the U.S.S.R.

When we turn back, remembering what this titanic ruler of millions told us, we hear in his voice frankness, strength of conviction and assurance, of course, of his power.

There were, however, discrepancies in his speeches; there was lack of knowledge of the American people and the American traditions. We heard him extol the fact that he was a miner's son and that Mikoyan was a carpenter's son. Why should he be extolling this simple and most natural fact taken for granted by us in the United States which was founded by carpenters, masons, farmers, preachers of all religions—people of the working class, carrying on for almost two centuries the refining process of democratic government? It was significant to hear him exult in his heritage because it showed that he was still living and fighting the ghostly enemies of a past era of aristocracy in the Czarist regime. He still is fighting non-existent imperial enemies —he cannot see any other country as democratic except the U.S.S.R. Our democracy is to him an unknown book because of his hypnotic involvement with imperialism. Through that barrier, through that block, he cannot see the United States as being much more highly advanced along the lines of democratic government than his own country.

It must have been incomprehensible to him to see farmer Garst shaking his fist at the reporters, shouting at them, and threatening them. It must have been incomprehensible to him to see the reporters piling on top of everything that had a top, freely trespassing all laws and regulations in order to give us first-hand impressions of our guest.

229

Khrushchev sees the United States of America as a stratified society, divided into classes; he does not see that it is a spiral or a ramp on which people can move back and forth and become whatever their desire and strength of vision prompt them to become.

There were so many blind spots of that nature which showed through his shrewd comments and his almost childish design to impress the American people!

His faithful interpreter, Oleg Troyanovsky, will also be missed by us of the United States. His brave, meticulous voice translated the words of Khrushchev with the precision of a fine mechanism; and to those who understand Russian it was amusing when Troyanovsky translated verbatim the drastic attacks on Khrushchev by the National Press Club president.

I thought at one time, while keenly listening, that Khrushchev was somewhat taken aback by the very precise translation of words and feeling faithfully transmitted to him by Troyanovsky. One could see the interpreter's absolute devotion to his master and to the government which he serves.

Khrushchev failed to grasp the democratic freedom of the United States which should have been obvious to him at every step he took on this ground. But it is not easy to discard the effects of the bitter revolutionary years which have made all the leaders of the Soviet Union forever ready for attack and consequent defense. Although nobody in the United States intended to minimize Russia's scientific success, he constantly boasted about the scientific achievements of his country.

What good is it doing us to increase our competition with the Russians, to invest billions of dollars on the perfection of machines to reach the moon? Would we be again struck with awe if after the Lunik the Russians sent up a Marsnik? What if we do learn of magnetic fields, or the lack of magnetic fields, on those planets while here on Earth we still live in intensified suspicion and mistrust?

At dinner in New York with Dorothy Liebes and her husband Relman Morin, who has been for years a top correspondent for the Associated Press, we talked of Khrushchev. We agreed that Khrushchev accomplished his mission which was to establish commerce between the United States and Russia.

"As to his statement regarding capitalism evolving out of feudalism, and communism out of capitalism, he took that directly from Lenin in 1904," Mr. Morin declared. "It was not his own conclusion. He docs not understand that an American in a small town in Pennsylvania is at the same time a land owner, a capitalist, and a worker in a factory. Khrushchev makes divisions where there are none. The American people are integrated individuals. You cannot pull them apart from a complex social system embodying many systems which do not conflict with one another.

"You could not begin to explain this to Khrushchev. He thinks in terms of stratified social systems. It is true that the U.S.S.R. is stratified communism. This thought is correct. America, however, is free of any stratification—this he cannot understand."

Relman Morin is a highly respected newspaperman. His reporting on the Little Rock troubles won him a prize. He is tall and bears a strong resemblance to President Eisenhower with as dignified a bearing.

His wife, Dorothy Liebes, America's foremost designer of fabrics, is also tall, blonde and handsome. She loves her work as a creative designer and weaver, and she has revolutionized the whole field. By her individual use of materials in fabrics, she freed the rigid standards of weaving. Her work is always imaginative.

Dorothy Liebes designs and makes fabrics for Du-Pont. She has supplied materials not only for house furnishings, but for industry as well—air lines, steamships, automobiles, restaurants, theaters. Her colors are bold yet harmonious. Freely using gold and silver, she was the first to introduce metallic thread in fabrics. Dorothy Liebes uses any material she feels will give a beautiful texture and was among the first to introduce texture in fabrics. Mr. Wright liked her work.

Years ago, shortly after my daughter Svetlana's death, Dorothy Liebes came to the desert to inspire me once more to weave. I had woven for some years, learning by my own experience.

I remember so well Dorothy sitting on our Sun Terrace with her golden hair coiled in doubled braids about her head like a crown. She worked the loom and shuttle with the precision and feeling of a musician playing a fine musical instrument. She spoke of various techniques of weaving—of beauty of colors and new textures. She did all of this for me with love and understanding of my loss.

William T. Evjue, the editor and publisher of the Madison *Capital Times,* acts in a straightforward fashion based on justice and fairness. He defends the rights

of his state and his country. He is one of the very few
great editors today who uphold the rights of the individual regardless of party affiliations. He is severe with
political sinners and does not hesitate to plunge one of
them into the cold water of oblivion. He stands for
these great ideals of democracy: freedom of speech,
sovereignty of the individual; and above all he believes
that people should know the truth no matter how hard
it may be at times to accept it. If we know truth, we
will know how to act; otherwise we will be caught
unprepared. We need more men of Mr. Evjue's caliber
to help us see the course of our contemporary history
and the dangers that threaten us on this course. King
Olaf of Norway has bestowed the Cross of Merit on
this great editor. I am proud to be working for his newspaper.

I am rapidly beginning to bear the marks of a newspaperwoman—I defend my paper, my editor, my readers. As far as I am concerned, there is no better editor,
no better paper, and there are no better readers. At the
remotest slight in reference to any of these three, I find
myself rising in indignant rage.

Where can you find a stronger editor who fights for
the right of every American to know what goes on in
his country? And where can you find a better staff of
writers and reporters, of whom I now am one? Who
ever had more appreciative readers than the readers
of my column? I receive letters from friends and acquaintances and from those I have not had the privilege of meeting who enjoy sharing with me the events
of my life. There is not one group of people anywhere
among whom there will not be some who will think

233

with me, feel with me, smile with me, and at times even laugh with me.

When Mr. Wright and I went to New York I felt that something was incomplete if there was no copy of the *Capital Times* around. When the bellboy brought a roll of them up to our apartment, I quickly grabbed it and both Mr. Wright and I immediately sat down and read the *Capital Times* before we reached for the local *New York Times*.

Yes, I bear all the marks of a newspaperwoman.

Some time ago Mr. Wright was invited by our friend, Robert Moses, New York Park Commissioner, to speak at a meeting and luncheon given by the committee for slum clearance. I was not invited. I quickly telephoned to my editor Mr. Evjue to please send me a press card so that as a credentialed newspaperwoman I could attend an event that I thought would be interesting to my readers. Such an act in the past would have been incredible on my part. I received the card and was informed that I could be present at the luncheon which, however, unfortunately had to be cancelled because of terrible weather conditions.

I have come to understand what tremendous work goes into making up a newspaper. I have come to understand the hardships, the anxieties, the concentration that is back of every reporter's article. And I understand the editor's high responsibility to organize the material and to consolidate it all and present his newspaper to the readers as the highest medium of communicating the pulse of his country.

We have known Mr. Evjue since the time when our position in society was precarious, when Mr. Wright had very little work, and when he was recognized but by few, as a great architect. Mr. Evjue became a friend and supporter of Mr. Wright as a person and of his architecture as indigenous American architecture. Through our difficulties, financial failures, social barriers, Mr. and Mrs. Evjue were not only our friends but they also befriended our young people, the aspiring architects. They never changed during those years of hard life and, when fame and success followed, the friendship remained marked by mutual understanding and respect. It is particularly valuable to me because I too have experienced as others have, that friends are scarce during difficult years and friends are plentiful in years of plenty. We appreciated our friends especially when we started the Taliesin Fellowship, those who stood by us through trials and attacks on our methods of education.

We still are not completely free from those attacks but we stand stronger, on firmer ground backed by twenty-seven years of experience in this new form of teaching. So now, when our work is written about, spoken about on the radio and presented on television, when it has been accepted throughout the whole world, we look back with warmth to those friends that endorsed us before the world did. In the rapidly changing values of political, social, economic orders prevalent in the world today, a friendship held high appears as an indispensable life-line for a hopeful future. We are all affected by these social and scientific changes, and to determine whether they are for the better or for the worse in our future, our measure remains the presence of integrity and dignity in human relations.

Elizabeth Gordon, the Editor of *House Beautiful,* has always been a great admirer of Mr. Wright and his work. I had dinner with her one day at New York's "Whiskey Building"—Seagram's. We walked into the most costly, most famous, most spectacular restaurant of the great metropolis—The Four Seasons. Three huge Miró tapestries hung on the three walls of the foyer. Between the two restaurants upstairs we were faced by a brassy tapestry of Picasso.

We entered the high-ceilinged dining room of silky wood-paneled walls. Two of the walls were entirely of windows from floor to ceiling. Over the glass were strung thin chains of silver and brass. These were in constant, delicate motion.

We were told that this phenomenon was caused by the current of air below the glass. The continuous gentle movement was very effective. Beautiful mobiles of light plastic in gold and silver were suspended vertically from the ceiling in trembling motion—reminding us of some aspects of the Northern lights.

Miss Gordon ordered dinner for us, complete from *hors d'oeuvres* to dessert. It was all especially selected by Mr. Joseph Baum who runs the restaurant. Miss Gordon has given them the support of her appreciation from the very beginning.

"Because," she said, "I saw they were in earnest—getting the best and the finest of everything. They even have their own herb gardens out of the city. They study each course and investigate every brand of wine that should go with it. They are really dedicated people."

Elizabeth Gordon is an extraordinary woman with an extraordinary career. She is tall, with light fair skin and blue eyes—very feminine, with a most productive and practical mind; restless, with an unceasing flow of good ideas.

When she was a student at Northwestern University in Evanston, Illinois, still in her teens, she suddenly conceived an idea as she walked by an automobile showroom on Michigan Avenue and saw a new model of the Stutz Bearcat painted snow white displayed in the window. The following Saturday morning she dressed in her best and, looking very fashionable, walked into the office of the car's distributor and asked to see the manager.

"I know how to increase the sale of your cars," she said. "I am a university student. If you will let me drive your white roadster on the campus and around town, I will sell lots of them for you—faster than you can get them."

The manager looked at this attractive smart girl, smiled broadly, shook her hand and said, "Come back on Monday and you can take the car."

Miss Gordon called up a friend, told him what happened, and asked him to teach her how to drive a car over the week end. She spent hours learning to drive, returned on Monday morning, and for the remainder of the year drove the exciting white Bearcat around the streets of Evanston and Chicago. She had enormous luck in selling the cars to sophisticated co-eds while the happy manager marveled at the wit of this astute and astonishing young woman.

Early in her career as Editor of *House Beautiful*.

Miss Gordon was asked to speak to a convention of the Lumbermen's Association. She had heard that many of these businessmen were displeased that a woman should be asked to "tell them how to run their business." When she came into the room, dressed as usual in chic original clothes, there was a murmur of discontent and antagonistic glances were directed toward her.

She went to the platform, and when three men openly objected to her presence there, she simply invited them to come to the platform and discuss the lumber situation with her in an open forum. The atmosphere among the rest of the lumbermen suddenly changed. They now wanted to protect this lovely young woman!

However, she handled the forum superbly. The entire association was delighted and applauded unanimously. Elizabeth Gordon then told them that the three men who openly objected to her were her friends! That was her idea. They applauded more furiously than before.

Elizabeth Gordon spins ideas for *House Beautiful* effortlessly. The magazine has a circulation of about three-quarters of a million, and it is a persuasive force in American design. She lives and breathes her work, while looking beautiful, tender and fragile as an Eighteenth Century Watteau watercolor.

Recently I was discussing various friends and acquaintances with Mary Lou and Harold C. Price, our friends and clients of Bartlesville, Oklahoma; and Mary

Lou said, "People are what they are inside. Education doesn't really change them."

"But," I remarked, "it puts on them a veneer which temporarily gives us an entirely different picture of what they are."

"That's true, but sooner or later they will show their real nature," Mrs. Price reflected.

Wealth often effects more serious changes than education. I have seen people assume different attitudes once they either gradually or suddenly become aware of money as their power. But Mary Lou and Harold Price have not changed their natural love of life and people, their appreciation of society and its values nor their kindness toward their friends whom they have kept for a lifetime.

In the beginning of their marriage attractive blue-eyed Mary Lou Price was a modest school teacher in the town of Bartlesville, and Mr. Price who had graduated from the Colorado School of Mines had an electric welding shop. Because Harold Price often was gone for long months at a time on field work, they went through hardships of separation, especially during the first years of their marriage. Electric welding was not much in use in 1921 and many people thought it would never replace acetylene welding.

"The first welding machine would not make 'juice'," they reminisced. "We hooked it up backwards! Our first pipeline leaked in every joint. We had not had enough experience."

But the new Harold C. Price Company had faith and after adding seven years of experience they welded storage tanks on contract. Those jobs included welding steel bottoms and roofs on tanks throughout the midcontinent area. Over the years they kept improving the technique, and since 1928 they have cut the cost of welding the pipelines over forty per cent.

Their sensational war project, Canol, abbreviated from Canadian Oil, was considered one of the greatest construction feats in the history of the oil industry. "When we teamed to form the Bechtel-Price-Callahan Company we knew the job was going to be tough—and supremely important. The Canol project was in the rugged territory across the Continental Divide in Canada and Alaska.

"Twenty-five thousand men worked on Canol in temperatures that sometimes reached 50° below zero. In twenty months we succeeded in conquering an undeveloped area one-third the size of the United States, building 2,000 miles of road through the wilderness, laying 1,700 miles of pipeline, building a refinery at Whitehorse, and transporting thousand of workmen and tons of materials to the job a thousand miles from civilization." That certainly was a feat.

Then there is the Big Inch, a pipeline which carries oil from the Gulf Coast to consuming centers on the Atlantic seaboard.

During the war the Price Company rendered its services to the war effort. They supplied foremen and welders to Calship, Terminal Island, California, where 200 Liberty ships were launched in less than four years, and to Marinship, Sausalito, California, where they turned out Liberty freighters, fleet oilers and T-2 tankers—in record quantities—and to the Evansville shipyard in Indiana, in which more LST's were produced than in any other shipyard in the world.

In the rugged terrain of eastern Kentucky, they had

to lay a line directly up the sides of steep mountains where they graded cliffs to provide a usable right of way. Pipe-stringing trucks had to be towed by tractors.

When Mr. and Mrs. Price and their two sons, Harold and Joe, who are also in the business, speak of Canol, the Big Inch and the Little Big Inch, their faces glow with warmth and the sentiment of living experiences:

"When the spring comes it is like a spring fever with the pipeliners, and at the first call to start the migration to the job, they and their wives and children are excited over the new adventure which may take them into the swamps of Louisiana, the craggy mountains of western Kentucky or into the tropics of Venezuela.

"Out they go in a big migration—400 men and their families on one section. They park the trailers near some central point or town where their children go to school while their fathers dig the ditches in which they lower pipelines, welding them and protecting them from corrosion by the earth's elements. After the long stretch is finished they move their families on to the next central town where again the great adventure of a pipeliner's work takes them."

When Mrs. Price once visited a location and was staying in a small town nearby, the grocery man asked her, "What I can't get is how do those rough-living pipeliners drive Cadillacs?"

Mrs. Price spoke proudly, "They have enough money to retire any time they wish. Their jobs pay them well; they own ranches and farms, but they just cannot give up the adventure of pipelining. It is like the pioneering days of America experienced every spring all over again. Once a pipeliner always a pipeliner!"

The work that the H. C. Price Company does is

241

gigantic. But to Mr. and Mrs. Price and their sons, laying the gushing arteries in the earth is science, adventure, romance and, above all, service to mankind.

Mr. Wright always appreciated the work of Edward Durell Stone and also enjoyed him as a friend. "Ed is honest," he said. "His architecture is honest, too."

Mr. Wright told me that Ed Stone's Embassy building in New Delhi was the most beautiful building in India. He hoped that Mr. Stone's work would awaken India to an appreciation of fine architecture.

Edward Stone is married to the gorgeous Maria, an outspoken, frank, quick-minded young woman. "Be careful, it is difficult to be beautiful, and quite dangerous," I said to her once.

She agreed wholeheartedly. "I did not think of it but you are right. People think that if a woman is pretty she cannot possess an intellect. A pretty woman has to convince people of her intelligence."

But I do not think that Maria Stone has to work hard at it. We spoke of present-day architects and her statements ripped the more bizarre current ones with masterly skill—there was not much left of them when she finished. She gave me some good warning regarding a California architect. "I would not trust him a second—he would stoop to nothing to get a job—he would snatch it out of your hands while you believed that the job was yours," her large black eyes flashed with gaiety, humor and common sense.

242

She is devoted to her husband and loyally protects him like a young tigress. Ed Stone takes her as a God-given gift—he worships everything about her. When Mr. Wright and I invited them to dinner in New York one night he was unusually quiet. "Mr. Stone," I said, "you have barely spoken tonight."

"Well, you see, Mrs. Wright, remember last time we had dinner with you and Mr. Wright? When we got home Maria scolded me for talking too much. She said I did not give her a chance to hear what Mr. Wright had to say. So tonight I shut up." His eyes shone with pleasure while his wife shook her head with a bewitching smile.

It is refreshing to be with this married couple who are always aware of each other's presence. It is much too often that a marriage becomes an habituated relationship in which husband and wife are aware of everyone except each other. So naturally they lose contact in a social gathering. At home they find no necessity to maintain the social conduct and attitude they so lavishly display with others, and soon the relationship becomes condensed into an automatic repetitious pattern of the same words—"Would you turn the light out?" "Where are my socks that match? You got them mixed up again!" "Did you get my shirts from the laundry?" Or: "I need money for new curtains." "The children need new shoes." "The dentist's bill must be paid this week." "Bobby has a stomach ache." And so on.

Granted that all this is necessary, the relationship should not be allowed to reduce itself to such repetitious patterns. Some of the social grace, some touch of poetry must be maintained as part of married life to prevent the gradual sterilization of love. And marriage without love is a wasteful crime that could be so easily avoided. The pattern of necessities in work and life together does not exclude the possibility of maintaining personal interest in each other. How many times the wife neglects the husband for the children, or the husband neglects the wife for his work or his associates. Then one day, unnoticed by either of them, they find they have grown apart from each other.

There can be maintained a balance in all life provided there is an enlightened recognition of the danger that we face in losing that which we live by—love.

On a non-stop flight from New York to Phoenix late in 1959, I met T. R. Robsjohn-Gibbings, the writer and interior designer, whose books *Goodbye Mr. Chippendale, Mona Lisa's Mustache,* and *Homes of the Brave* have received wide acclaim; we talked at length.

Mr. Wright and I always enjoyed his quick, highly polished wit. He admired Mr. Wright and understood his work.

"The Internationalist architects were afraid of Mr. Wright," he said. "They fought him with every conceivable method. They all wanted the easy way of promoting their architectural thesis which was to make architecture academic, establish a style, and teach it in formulas binding the masses with architectural chains. That way their following was easy to establish and they could become leaders in the architectural field.

"But what to do with Mr. Wright? He was a menace to them because he proclaimed and practiced the principle of Organic Architecture, which would make architecture free of chains. With this principle, Mr. Wright freed the individual to build according to his own gift —on sound ground without the bondage of academic style.

"The Internationalist group attempted to tag Mr. Wright as a Romanticist, but it did them no good. They tried to date him—it did them no good. He went ahead on his noble way and now this latest terrific building— the Guggenheim Museum."

"Yes," I said, "Mr. Wright knocked all their architectural props from under them. They have fallen on their faces. The building is a revelation of the most advanced architectural thought. This building liberated all the museums in the world from the clichés which made them mere crates for works of art.

"The lovers of art will now see paintings and sculpture as Mr. Wright intended them to be seen—in a harmonious relationship with the building—so simple and natural an idea and yet so difficult to comprehend for the Museum Director, James Sweeney. It is appalling the way he impaled the paintings on metal rods to separate them from the walls, violating the very principle Mr. Wright fought for."

When I asked Mr. Robsjohn-Gibbings what he thought of Picasso, he answered, "People of all ages have dreamed of a land beyond their own. So when some more adventurous merchants traveled to a distant country, they brought back with them influences from their impressions. For instance, when the Romans went to Egypt, they brought back with them Egyptian collections of art which influenced Roman civilization. Then later in history the French traveled to China and brought back with them the Chinese art which influenced French forms of art. It was called *La Chinoiserie.*

"In modern times when people traveled to the African jungles, they were stirred by various primitive tribal religious ceremonies. They were particularly impressed by some sects which, in order to produce a tense emotional state in the tribe, distorted natural and familiar objects—a lion, a crocodile, or a man—carved or painted on wood.

"Those symbols were necessary for their life. They helped the primitives to feel supernatural forces more intensely. But when Picasso and other painters practiced the same distortion, in our time, it naturally had no place because we do not need that kind of symbol to represent us. It belongs to the primitive tribes of the African jungle. It is foolish to claim that such distorted paintings are the reflection of our unhappy civilization."

"I am glad to hear you say this because both Mr. Wright and I felt the same way about the ugliness that passes for modern expression of our life," I said. "Beauty is pushed away by the distortionists as old-fashioned. But they cannot kill it—as they cannot kill the great ideas that Mr. Wright has sent out to generate a creative force in the world for centuries to come."

Our friend, Walter Reed Bimson is the Chairman of the Valley National Bank in Phoenix, and his name is synonymous with Phoenix. It is due to his vision, courage and implacable business sense, more than to anyone else's, that Phoenix has grown from a bleak western town into a prosperous, booming city.

He is endowed with a force, understanding, kindness and vision that has won over human frailties and even betrayals. At an early age Walter Bimson learned that impulsive trust may lead to financial loss. He wanted to go to M.I.T. to become an architect and, to fulfill this wish, joined a group of young people who were selling books on the west coast during the summer months. He successfully received deposits for the book subscriptions, but before the time came to deliver the books and collect the rest of the money—his share was $400—he had to go east to register at M.I.T. and he asked his friend to collect for him. The "friend" collected. Mr. Bimson never saw him again.

Instead of being disillusioned in human nature, he registered this experience as a valuable lesson only. Now, having no money, he had to go to work for four years as a minor employee in a bank in his home town of Berthoud, Colorado, and for twelve years in the Harris Trust and Savings Bank in Chicago. He had so many good ideas that at the end of four years in Berthoud they were worried that he would own the bank; and he was well on the way to accomplishing this in the Harris Trust.

When offered the post of President in a Phoenix bank in 1933, the year of the depression, he leaped at the chance because he felt he could now put his ideas and experience into action. He immediately proceeded to reorganize and revolutionize the bank. While all other banks were refusing loans, Walter Bimson encouraged loans. Pretty soon he was known in Phoenix as a friend of all those who truly wanted to re-establish themselves and start a new business after the crushing blow of the depression. He personally appraised individuals and, sensing their potentialities, loaned them money without securities.

There was a young carpenter who started on his way to Arizona with one hundred dollars. When he arrived he had sixty dollars left, but he had plenty of good ideas. He wanted to start a construction company of his own. At the beginning of World War II, he saw his chance and bid on a government job. But he needed $150,000. No one else would loan him this sum. Walter Bimson did. This man in a few years was doing a multi-million dollar business. He is Del E. Webb, half owner of the New York Yankees.

Walter Bimson's offices in Phoenix were on the first floor of the bank for many years and anyone wanting to see Mr. Bimson, no matter how humble, could walk right in. The story goes that, many times when ranchers drove in to Phoenix from far-away ranches, the first thing they did was to take their families to the bank until his place teemed with a constant stream of visitors. If he was busy talking to some powerful capitalist-client, they would simply walk around the offices and show their families the paintings on the walls and chat with each other.

As the years went by and the progress of the bank continued, Walter Bimson was forced to move to an upper floor if he wished to do any work at all. But even there he is still besieged with a flow of visitors who want to shake the hand of Walter Bimson.

The bank has grown from six million dollars to almost 600 million dollars in deposits and the city of Phoenix has grown from a population of 48,000 to 364,000.

Among our friends in Paradise Valley it is known that it is Walter Bimson who has been largely responsible for the growth and development of Arizona's prosperity. Way back in 1933 he declared, "This state is going to be a great state some day. All it needs is a little encouragement."

And whatever money he loaned he made sure that it was good for Arizona as well as for those engaged in organizing a new business. He has helped us many times in the past.

What makes the fame of the fabulous Walter Bimson unusual is that during his twenty-seven years in Phoenix he has, without losing any money, benefited thousands of people by helping them get a start.

There are many legends built around the name of Walter Reed Bimson. He is a lover of art and likes to encourage young artists by buying their paintings. One day he showed us one of those extremely modern paintings he had bought. "I could not make head nor tails out of it," he said, "but that young man showed such real faith in himself and was so convinced that it was a good painting that I gave him a thousand dollars for it."

He admires able people and he perceives ability magically, at first sight. Having wanted to be an architect at one time, he follows the development of architecture with the eagerness of a young man.

His beautiful wife, Nancy, takes care of him with an abundance of cheerful persuasion. When taking out a little pillbox at the dinner table, he smiles benignly, "This is one of Nancy's suggestions," and takes the pills with a touch of the indulgent husband.

At the age of sixty-eight he is handsome, young. He and his Nancy are the most popular guests at all dinner parties. You can see them at the estates of great potentates as well as on simple picnics with the townspeople. They live much in their family—children and grandchildren.

On the day of our irreparable loss on April ninth, Walter and Nancy Bimson came to the services at six o'clock in the evening.

Late that night Wes and Gene heard footsteps coming down toward their rooms. In the midnight darkness they saw two silhouettes. They were Walter and Nancy Bimson. "We had to come back to reassure you of our complete confidence in you at Taliesin," Mr. Bimson said. "You have our backing. We are with you and we will help you in every way."

It is because of acts like these that legends are spun around the name of Walter Reed Bimson.

PART FOUR

REFLECTIONS

Chapter 12

(A talk to the Taliesin Fellowship)

I will read to you a part of Mr. Wright's talk on "The Nature of the Rose":

". . . See this lovely arrangement of roses on the table. To know this rose is to feel it first, of course, and enjoy and get out of it what it has to give and then pry into it for the source of satisfaction. What made it satisfying? What gave it charm? What was living in it—that is what you are after and pretty soon you will be on the track of what it is that gives life to nearly everything that is around you. What is the life of it? Then when you have mastered what is the life of that thing you are beginning to be able to put life into things yourself. You can make them live. Once you get at the source of the creation of the thing, *you can create it!*—in your way. Now that is the study of architecture, that is the study of art—reaching for the principle, mastering the principle . . ."

As you see, there is so much material to be taken, to be absorbed, to be digested, that it is difficult to grasp very much at one time. I will continue reading

253

to you every Sunday. We have inexhaustible material from a great and inspired mind. I wish that you would absorb this magnificent work not merely mentally but with all your system, in order that you in turn may live it.

Illumination is supposed to be a very rare experience that happens maybe once in a lifetime. But I believe that we can have many illuminations during our life. Sometimes we understand in a flash a thought, a problem, a complexity. We do not regard this as illumination, but it is. Many times we say, "How strange that I did not see this before—it is so very clear now." Such experiences are in the nature of illuminations. As Mr. Wright stated so simply, "To understand a thing is to love it"—that, too, is illumination. His life was a perpetual illumination.

If you felt the understanding, which is love, then everything in Nature, that is the whole of life, would appear entirely different. You would be ceaselessly discovering new forms at every turn of your life. At times the conditioning of our minds prevents us from spontaneous understanding. The first years in school condition us and standardize us. That is unavoidable with mass education. Later we must rid ourselves of this rigid pattern in order to return to the creative thinking with which we were endowed by Nature. And if we do not free our minds we get involved in formulas, dogmas, prejudices, and often fall victim to considering an insignificant fact of more importance than the safety of our interior world. We gradually lose the proper sense of values. Yet even if a shadow of a sorrow touches one, values are instantly transformed and we seek the treasures within. The world becomes many-dimensional, complex, conflicting; but at the same time there is always one direct channel—through understanding which circumscribes all. Union with Nature and understanding of its laws become among the greatest possessions a human being has.

Our former apprentice, Peter Berndtson, an architect from Pittsburgh, while visiting on June 8th remarked to me, "I have been away for many years but every time I come in contact with someone from Taliesin I continue right there where I left off. I feel no breach of time."

"Maybe it is because at Taliesin the relationship between people is real," I said. "There certainly cannot exist false fronts here. If they do exist, it is for a short time only. After a while the man shows what he is—he cannot help it. In the world you are in, the majority function on false fronts."

"That is true," Peter replied. "But what is so remarkable about it is that we here at Taliesin know each other very well, and we tolerate each other's weaknesses. But out in the world where I happen to be, not only do we live by false fronts but so often we don't tolerate one another as well."

Mr. Wright claimed that a true critic should be the man who appreciates the object he is criticizing instead of depreciating it. If you appreciate each other your criticism will be constructive and beneficent. If you depreciate one another the criticism will be a devastation of yourselves as individuals.

This will not happen at Taliesin, not if I can help it. And I think that we are pretty free of it. The criticism

255

of each other here is given with appreciation, understanding and patience—to a reasonable degree, of course.
When the weaknesses are damaging to our work, to our
ideal, we cannot tolerate them. But within limits, within reason, we do accept the fact that every human
being possesses weaknesses, and that there are no
angels walking on earth.

Chapter 13

(A talk to the 1959 National Convention of the Phi Beta Fraternity of Speech and Music, at Madison, Wisconsin)

Integration of the arts is manifest in the great Gothic cathedrals: architecture, music, sculpture, stained glass, and the magnificent robes of the priests became a complete whole. This was integration that occurred naturally. In those times the artists worked together, each an integral part of a great whole: the artists, great sculptors and painters, were satisfied and honored when they were able to fuse completely with the building, where they could express the spirit in material form. They were not personally engaged in promoting themselves. They simply contributed their efforts and liked the process of their work. What they experienced and saw and what they gave to others was sufficient for them. We have lost or perhaps we never knew, the names of many of those great people.

In Notre Dame of Paris, a cathedral 800 years old, we find a correlation of arts. Even philosophy was integrated in terms of sculpture. The vicious chimeras or gargoyles of Notre Dame express scorn, rage and ignorance, from which man must free himself. Among the powerful chimeras that seem to jeer at the city, there stands the slim figure of an angel. The angel is passive, his trumpet is lowered and his face is very wise—self-contained. One feels that he can raise the trumpet at any moment and the chimeras will vanish into space and dissolve into nothingness. This has been so highly expressed in abstract sculptural form that it speaks a whole philosophy. Through civilization and through our necessity to apply ourselves to mechanical progress we have almost lost such integration of art.

At Taliesin Mr. Wright and I tried to create some new form of that same spirit of ancient times. In our life now we try to integrate achitecture, poetry, painting, sculpture, music, dance and speech. I do not believe there was a better speaker than Mr. Wright, who expressed himself in an eloquent, articulate and original way.

I would like to see born a Society of Integrated Arts. There is a wide separation between the arts now and none of them ever speaks to another, nor do they ever reach one another on any common ground.

Philosophy, too, like music, painting, sculpture, poetry, is a separate department. I believe that all can be one. I cannot say that we have already perfected this at Taliesin because no one achieves perfection on earth, but we are striving in the direction of integrating the arts.

The philosopher usually cares little about music or other forms of the arts; the architect is not much interested in philosophy, poetry or dance; the musician knows little of literature or the architecture of the world; the painter needs architectural training because it is imperative for him to know the structure of what he paints—yet in reality he knows little of structure.

The great painter, Leonardo da Vinci, not only knew the structure of the human body, he knew science, philosophy, architecture, sculpture and expressed this knowledge in everything he created.

In our time we are enlightened through a greater creative force in the genius of Frank Lloyd Wright. He was a complete man—the symbol of Life and Art integrated.

And it is this development of completeness we need today. Integration of the arts is the way to fight the specialist, segregated from others and therefore segregated from life, because life is truly the greatest integration we know. The more we blend with one another, the more we commune with one another in this country and with other countries of the world, the closer we will approach integration of the whole world.

"Arts are expression of eternity," Mr. Wright has said. Creative man is the one who feels a deeply religious quality. It is only through our mechanical civilization that some of this precious quality has been diverted from its course of development, submerged by our mode of life. We had to live and we had to make compromises. But compromise made once or twice should not necessarily follow us all our life. And certainly it should not be allowed to affect our faith in arts as an expression of eternity.

To achieve this in the best way possible one must try to free oneself from the chains of civilization. On the one hand civilization has done a great deal of good for us—on the other, it has bound us.

In the hurry of our life many a magnificent thought, many an idea, goes unexpressed. We live in a world of concrete forms and we cannot turn our backs on that world. And no matter how discouraged we may become because we fail to express those ideas, we cannot go into exile from the world. Contribute we must at all cost toward its progress.

Japan is one of the cultures from which we could learn a great deal. Mr. Wright told me that even the poorest coolie in Japan in his little house has always some work of art—a lacquer bowl, a little flower arrangement—that stands in just the right place. The Japanese hold beauty in high esteem and believe that life should not be deprived of it at any time. Beauty and spirit are one. If life is deprived of beauty, great damage is done. We must keep in motion just as the plant grows, moving to the flowering, to the fruition, to the seed. There must be no stops. We must never say to ourselves: "I am satisfied. Now I have it. I have achieved what I wanted to achieve. Now I can take it easy." Never.

There must be no such thing, because a stop like that is a dangerous interruption of continuity. We all will come to our final Stop but we have the choice of moving upgrade or downgrade toward it—certainly we should not induce it before its time by arresting our inner growth.

In the true expression of ourselves we are about as close to divinity as we can get.

I have some groups that I teach who do not live at Taliesin. To those who have families, I suggest that they find some musical instrument, like the recorder, which is inexpensive and easy to learn to play. The children also learn quickly and the whole family has fun playing together. I ask the parents to paint with their children. Such forms of self-expression create another dimension in what might otherwise be a drab life.

Many of them have done very well. They have created integration in their lives so they no longer need to go elsewhere in order to find relaxation and pleasure.

It is not easy to achieve the true and beautiful expression of oneself. This must be sought with persistence because too much pressure, too much technical activity and preoccupation with modern gadgetry have complicated our lives. Acceleration of tempo from outside has slowed down our interior life. We have little time for literature and rely upon the current magazines only to find that we are neither enlightened nor even informed correctly. How many times after you have finished such reading have you asked yourself, "What did I get out of it?" And you know that you are no better off then you were before.

There should always be the creative element in life. We have to make it ourselves, woven out of our own spirit—then it has meaning. We cannot depend altogether upon exterior circumstances. The simplest form of expression, even the arrangement of a room, contains a creative element and can be raised to excellence.

Chapter 14

Volumes in many languages have been written about Mr. Wright, his architecture and the Taliesin Fellowship. But one of the mildly fashionable architects of the International style who has been an off-and-on admirer of Mr. Wright's work takes the prize.

He has put himself in print, rolling with pleasure in his misconception, about Mr. Wright, his architecture and the principle upon which the Taliesin Fellowship is based. The architecture of Mr. Wright and the Taliesin way of life are incomprehensible to him. He believes that a real gentleman never dips his hands into soapy dishwater, or holds a hammer and nails, or chops wood for a fire.

No, he belongs to the new class of "art-intelligentsia" whose only physical exertion is holding a pencil or a pen. Even eating is, after all, a rather vulgar, exhausting, but necessary habit.

Now, how have the members of this section of our society representing this new class benefited humanity? From the tip of their lead pencil drips the sterile style of accomplished sycophants; they but skim the surface of organic ideas in Mr. Wright's architecture and turn them into a formula—the same for all their buildings. Always standing on stilts, their buildings are dangerously beglassed from top to bottom, without sense, necessity, grace, style or character. This new class is hot on the trail of sensationalism.

Our Taliesin children at the age of nine draw such buildings without effort, and put more character into them than the International stylists do.

One can project a creative spirit into all work, as we do at Taliesin, from chores to construction, from the garden and the farm to playing the violin, singing Palestrina and working at the drafting board. It is in this enormous scale of action that talent and capabilities are exercised freely. It is thus that the imagination is stimulated into production in terms of life. Such an ideal, of course, is beyond the understanding of this new crop of designers who know little or nothing of the sound structural engineering that marks every building which Mr. Wright has built. They only copy the surface lines without knowledge, using them senselessly.

Yet, this new crop is not a negligible quantity. It is by no means harmless, because it slips into important places of authority and corrupts generations of men by artificial dictates of artificial principle for an artificial life.

Yes, they are harmful because they possess the power of the wealthy who look up to them for counsel in the choice of works of art, houses to live in and the interior decorating of their apartments. Internationalism is slowly creeping throughout the whole world. Europe, Asia, South America, Africa, and now America, are being robbed of any natural expression of their culture.

The tall piles of glass and steel forced upon the world are actually "machines to live in"—to quote one of the Internationalist architects.

A New York woman told me, "I want to have the kind of house that in every room I can turn on the hose and wash clean the furniture, work of art, floor, ceiling, and walls. I want everything in it waterproof. I don't care what it looks like!"

This is but one harmful effect of the Internationalist style on the culture of the world; and, of course, it goes hand in hand now with the emphasis put upon science—the two are a great threat to the preservation of our spirit. A so mechanized world will gradually produce mechanized human beings. New York is already crushing the life of the spirit, walling it in, by its menacing skyscrapers where diminutive human figures try to make their fight against this threat to spiritual survival.

Faith in man and his immortality—the antithesis of this so-called "Internationalism"—will help us fight this new blight descending on us, ripping our spirit. Science negates the spirit; we must become aware of this new danger as Satan attempting to leave us at the mercy of the mind alone—cold, mechanical, without the love needed to make our existence on earth meaningful.

The current thought of the "art intelligentsia" concerning creative artists is that they need not be ethical individuals. As long as they create works of art it is supposedly none of our concern what they are ethically. To condone the conduct of some artists in such a way will eventually cause great harm to our society. We are living in precarious times. On one side we are faced by science's cold, inimical-to-life march, and on the other by the irresponsible cavortings of "artists."

Faith is our only hope. To protect ourselves from destruction by both these swiftly onrushing tendencies, we—society—must demand development along the line of spirit in both science and art. We must no longer allow them to follow their own hazardous tracks, leaving us at their mercy.

The time has come when the spirit of man must be regarded more highly than either science or art. Science is giving us mere mechanical power; perverted art is giving us degenerate forms, devoid of sense, harmony and beauty. Science celebrates new found forms of destruction; perverted art celebrates new found forms of ugliness.

We must be aware of this fearsome picture of our civilization. We must maintain our faith, upholding the spirit of man as the highest form of expression, and allowing neither science nor mistaken "art" to trample it under foot.

A scientist without religion and an artist without religion are both dangerous to society. Unfortunately, they seem now to be in the lead; to follow them is to destroy ourselves. Yes, the time has come for us to adhere more strongly than ever to our faith.

We could introduce in our schools daily classes in religion as we have in mathematics and we should consider them to be at least as important as mathematics. The differences between religious denominations could be resolved by calling a council of representatives of each denomination to agree upon a method of teaching which would deal with the fundamental basis of religion without conflicting with any special branch. After all we must not forget that God is One for us all in spite of sectarianism. We could convey to our children the presence of God above all branches of religion. If we develop in our children a highly ethical religious sense, perhaps we can survive the devastating tendencies of destructives forces today.

The tendencies are frightful. Opening the pages of any magazine one reads of the new degenerate, drunken writers who seem to delight in the exhibition of drunkenness, and the new crop of authors, especially women, who happily narrate the sordid experiences of their lives. These are typical latter-day writers. Most of them mock at the human spirit, exude passionless sensuality and the click of the cold machine brain which now seems to be a mere motor attached to the neck of man.

In any city of the world today there is little in art that is worth seeing. The galleries are full of lurid exhibitions of morbid landscapes. Beauty is classified as sentimentality, an old-fashioned left-over in a bleak blanched world of cold utilitarian realism gnashing its teeth at all spiritual value.

Chapter 15

Science keeps finding new uses for old drugs; among the recent ones, novocaine, which now has found its way in helping arthritis, arteriosclerosis and other kinds of ailments, especially in the aged.

A recent article describes how a woman of ninety, after taking intravenous novocaine injections, is at the age of a hundred running agilely up and down stairs!

Novocaine tests were made on 5,000 people in Bucharest alone. In 1951 a doctor started giving injections to twenty-five people between the ages of sixty and ninety-nine and the results were all good. Even younger people with some skin irritations which no one could cure were greatly relieved by novocaine injections.

Always being interested in new discoveries along all lines that can help us in our transit on earth, I talked about it to our doctors who immediately sent for medical journals and found that the only available literature at the time was in the German language.

We had staying with us Dr. Joseph Rorke from Pennsylvania who became interested in the way of life at Taliesin and started his practice in Scottsdale, Arizona, about 12 miles from Taliesin West. His wife and daughter lived with us; Mrs. Rorke studied music, dance and interior decorating at Taliesin. They planned to build a home designed by the Taliesin Associated Architects.

At one of our Saturday evenings in the theater, we had our Chinese architect, Ling Po, and his mother, Madame Po, for dinner. Ling Po overheard me speaking with Dr. Rorke about the new possibilities of the use of novocaine. The next day, Ling Po asked Dr. Rorke for an appointment. "My mother and I wish to present ourselves to you for your novocaine injections experiment, please," he stated gravely. "I wish you to try it on my mother and me before you try it on Mr. and Mrs. Wright."

Dr. Rorke smiled kindly saying, "We have not come to that point as yet. I am merely investigating the literature on this subject. Thank you just the same."

Some time later I read about a new "solution" for the treatment of high-strung children. Gerald O'Gorman, a doctor at Smiths Hospital in England, placed "higher-grade mentally defective young women" with these children as their companions. They were mentally the same age as the children. They were allowed to express their maternal instincts, hugging and kissing and fondling the children, going to bed with them, and lulling them to sleep. It was said this was a great help to ten worn-out nurses, who before then had not been able to make the children do anything!

Suppose the children are calmed down in that manner—what of their future? What would their attitude be toward adults later on? Since their big, strong, motherly playmates are on the same mental level with them, the children would undoubtedly soon learn how to rule them. The care of intelligent but high-strung children by mentally defective adults seems to me a monstrous idea which would cause terrible repercussions in the future.

The most valuable trait in a doctor, one he cannot get from medical books, is common sense. Only when common sense in a doctor is combined with his medical information is he really worthy of being called a doctor. Even if he possesses vision and intelligence, without common sense to balance them he cannot be a truly good doctor. In experimenting with new ideas he must have common sense; if he lacks it he will be lost in mere theory. Though he may give temporary relief he may cause irreparable damage, since each human being presents a new problem. It is common sense that will tell him that prescribing alike for all is a too easy, and most uncertain, way out. But it is rare to find a doctor who still gives sufficient individual attention to each patient. The usual doctor is overloaded with work to such a degree that he has little time left even to keep up with current medical research.

This precious ingredient, common sense, is often lacking not only in the practice of medicine but in the daily "educated" life of all of us.

Civilization does, without doubt, injure some of the inherent, natural attributes in a human being. Too much development along the ruts of the mind confuses, cripples, or negates common sense. The correct solution of a problem is based primarily on common sense which serves as a balance wheel to our judgment.

The cigarette scare seems to be shared equally by manufacturers and customers. The manufacturers fear financial loss; the consumers fear the loss of pleasure. The only members of the population that seem happy over the cigarette scare are the analytical specialists. Their business is booming. The increase of the cigarette-scared patients has been so enormous of late that many specialists are taking trips to Japan, to China, even to the mountains of Afghanistan, "to rest their overworked nerves."

Based on the rumors I have heard I will attempt to create a "scientific" account of the plight of our civilization. I can introduce this account by an example of the condition of my dog ZaZa. Our good Dr. Micuda of the Phoenix Kindness Hospital told me, "Mrs. Wright, if your dog were a human I would tell her to smoke to ease her shattered nerves—as it is, I can only give her a Miltown!"

The run of the mill "diagnosis" might well be as follows: "The psychological displacement due to abrupt ending of nicotine intake in an area of the system which is not supplemented by any other means of maintenance causes serious traumatic consequences"; or "a psychic urge taking an unhealthy mental channel based on lack of nicotine in the area of the brain is apt to develop a traumatic condition."

Should a happy marriage end in divorce the specialists could probably say, "Withdrawal of nicotine in the area of the central nervous system naturally results in traumatic attitudes toward one another"; or "traumatic signs of an occasional irresistible desire to slap each other is nothing more than nervous tension caused by lack of nicotine evaporation from the area of the chest operating the breathing apparatus."

The increase in the speed of speech at cocktail parties might prove that "the attendants suffer a pathological traumatic state due to a total disappearance of nicotine in certain gland areas, causing a jittery sensation."

So serious is the cigarette scare crisis, I hear, that there is even imminent danger of world war! Evidently the imbalance of nicotine-drained nervous cells in the area of New York City will result in the traumatic trance of the entire populace. They think too fast, they feel too fast, they speak too fast, and they no longer walk—they run! It would seem that everyone there lives in fear of some cataclysm on a gigantic scale.

Like other human beings, analytical specialists vary in their attitude toward the welfare of humanity. Some say, shrugging their shoulders, "Let them smoke. What's the difference! They will kill themselves some other way anyhow." Some take Omar Khayyam's philosophic approach to life, "Let them enjoy themselves while they can—the poor devils."

There are also the fanatical professional condemners of the cigarette-smoking habit as issuing not only from the chemical needs of the body but from the very center of a sinful soul. This by no means reduces their profitable living because they, too, are overburdened by cigarette-suffering sinners and they, too, have to leave for the Orient in quest of an area soothing to their overworked nerves. After having been soothed, they are charged for another crusade to save a traumatic generation from self-destruction.

271

But some fiercely defend the right of humanity to enjoy itself with wisdom, guiding nicotine-addicted men and women toward some healthy compromise which would not necessarily enrich the cigarette manufacturers but still keep them fairly comfortable.

According to the dictionary, "area" originally meant a level surface, a broad piece of level ground, a part of the earth's surface, etc., or vacant ground, region, tract, scope, range. The word has pervaded not only the world of mathematics and the military, but also of medicine. The dictionary further explains "area" as "a part of the cerebral cortex regarded as having a particular function. The projection areas are those parts having direct outside connections, through their projection fibers, with subcortical centers which in turn are connected with sense organs, muscles, etc. Those receiving afferent projection fibers are called sensory areas. They include the following: the acoustic, or auditory, area in the temporal lobe, the olfactory area . . . visual area . . . motor area . . . association areas."

However in the last few years this word has taken a grip on our mode of speech and now we seem unable to get along without it. We are addicted to it. We replace many a good word by this convenient substitute.

"Trauma" has not yet completely taken hold in our language but it is well on its way. "Trauma," the dictionary plainly says, is "an injury, wound, shock or the resulting condition . . . mental shock, a disturbing experience to which neurosis can be traced." But we are splurging with this word, following in the footsteps of our analytical specialists. For instance, if a husband injures his wife's feelings, he knowingly says, "The

272

trouble with you is that you are too touchy because of your traumatic condition." If a husband is sulking over some unjust criticism on the part of his mate, she in turn gives her scientific conclusion, "You, my dear, are suffering a bad case of trauma; that's all that's the matter with you." And if you, yourself, simply happen to be in a state of nervous tension, a friendly neighbor will happily reassure you of your "traumatic neurosis." And so the word becomes a means of insult.

It is curious to watch words creep into the language and in the course of time eventually lose their original meaning. Perhaps that is the way language is expanded. After the stage of being a mere fad is over, the word is eventually built solidly into the language, to be used naturally.

Some years ago, I had a friend possessed by diet-fads. "I want you to meet Marvin," she once said to me. Tall, swarthy Marvin stood on one side and grinned. "He used to be sick with bad colds all the time," she continued with animation. "We have just returned from the international convention of Anti-Meat-Eaters Society and Marvin was the star. He used to drink and smoke and gorge himself with rare beef and New York cut steaks and had headaches all the next day . . . Now he eats nothing but peanuts! He has not been sick a day since. All the nutriments he needs he gets from peanuts. It is really a remarkable thing what this diet did for Marvin!"

I looked at poor Marvin and thought with alarm, "Peanuts! Are we really going back to our remote ancestry that fast?" I did observe that dietitians are trying to return us to what they like to call "natural foods" but I did not think that we had reached that far back. I foolishly believed that we had evolved out of that kind of diet.

Richness and variety of foods are just as valuable, just as important to our state of well being as any other pleasure that God has offered us to enjoy on this earth. But the dietetic addicts are determined, under various banners and slogans, to march back in time.

Although some fundamental foods more or less agree with all of us, we do differ in our reactions to most foods, and to prescribe a certain diet as static pattern is unreasonable.

We had a guest at Taliesin who was an addict of Mr. Hauser's diet: blackstrap molasses, buttermilk, brown sugar and so forth. She was so full of theories that she actually did not observe that at Taliesin she was eating that very food. It passed by her because at every meal she was in the habit of expounding the virtues of Mr. Hauser's diet. Finally one day I pointed out to her that on the table we had everything that Mr. Hauser had and more that he had not even thought of.

In the course of this conversation she merely nodded absentmindedly and remained perfectly firm on her ground that Mr. Hauser was something entirely different. This addict to diet would eat a delicious luncheon with us but she did not know how to derive pleasure from eating. She was effusive about a recipe she had been reading while she ate unconsciously, not realizing that this was the very same dish.

With a little observation one notices that certain foods agree with one at times and not at other times.

274

For example, you find that two years ago you could eat cucumbers with great pleasure and no harm. This year cucumbers give you indigestion. Give them up and try them some other time. We change, and our interior conditions change accordingly. Our reactions, not only to food, but to everything around us, undergo change. And if we are sufficiently aware, we will know what we should do; I believe that the best physician one can consult is oneself. A good doctor will tell you this himself. He may have no time to study your particular system but he can give you sensible direction.

One can build a diet for oneself. It does not necessarily have to clash with any set rule. We have to adhere to some pattern of meals and time, and to a reasonable amount of basic foods like whole wheat or corn bread, brown sugar, buttermilk, honey, sorghum, oatmeal and fresh fruit and vegetables. Among them we can always choose those that are the best for us.

Auto-hypnotic power also has a great deal to do with our digestive system. Another friend told me that once while eating clams she had been mildly poisoned and had not been able to eat them since. I had forgotten about this and one evening we had clams in the soup which all of us thoroughly enjoyed. It was only when I went to bed that I was suddenly struck with anxiety: I had given my friend clams.

When she came to breakfast next morning I asked her fearfuly how she felt. "I feel fine and I always rest well at Taliesin," she responded. I did not tell her that morning. I thought that her hypnotic fixation might give her a delayed reaction and make her ill.

The following day I asked her, "Did you know that you ate clams the night before last?"

Even then, her face changed color. "Look," I said, "you needn't be frightened. You digested them beautifully. You are perfectly free to eat clams. Most probably something else gave you indigestion but every time you thought of clams you thought of pain and poison."

It is so simple for us to learn what foods are hard for us to digest at what time. This will naturally always vary. However, within our own range we can find the right way for ourselves. I do not believe that it is necessary to confine our enjoyment of food to the now fashionable raw liver, "tiger's milk," wheat germ or—peanuts.

Recently I read an illuminating article about the problem of the teen-ager. It told how many clever businessmen, through the grace of their dispensation as advertising kings, have caused adults to bend the knee before the teen-ager. These men claim that adults dress more and more like the teen-agers, read magazines the teen-agers like to read, look at moving pictures they enjoy, ride in cars they want to buy, type on typewriters they like. Adults imitate the language of the teen-agers, eat the food they prefer, drink their soft drinks—I hope soft—and the teen-agers even choose precious vacation spots for their parents. In other words adults are subjugated and enslaved, ruled by this new caste in America—the teen-ager. So we must not be surprised to read pretty soon that adults present a terrible social problem to the teen-ager. It is the teen-ager who will be consulting psychiatrists about the mental health of the adults; and the psychiatrist himself will be a mere teen-ager, who will set the rules and pattern for a good life for any adult past thirty.

It is easy to picture to oneself a dreary chain-gang of adults pulling a great financial load, with the teen-agers brandishing whips over them.

This is the advertisers' gruesome picture of the world which they so breathtakingly exploit. Most advertisements we see are the creations of just such "geniuses" who are hypnotizing the teen-agers into believing that they are the ruling class. Through repetitious appeal to their taste, playing on the chords of weak parenthood, these "geniuses" in the desperate attempt to find new markets are really the ones who are responsible for giving the teen-agers the imagined sense of supremacy. They send their "scouts" to find out from the lowest common denominator of teen-ager what he thinks he wants to wear, how he likes to have his typewriter designed, what kind of television programs he likes, and so on. Then the "scouts" scoot back to their sharp-minded "advertising geniuses" who contact the big companies and hypnotize them in turn into an advertising campaign to lure the vast body of teen-agers in America.

Doubtless this picture is true. Something basic has gone wrong in the parent-child relationship. The bond is weakening decidedly. Many an escape from drudgery that the parent takes to soon becomes a habit—whether it is excess in smoking or drinking or playing cards and so on. Addiction to anything is quickly seen by children, whose respect for the adults gradually diminishes. It is hard for a child to see his ideal in mother or father be crushed because he can so easily get them to do anything he wants them to do.

I remember once in the living room at Taliesin, I was sitting with a friend when her little boy aged eight came in. He went straight to Iovanna's harp and started drumming its strings any which way. I could hardly hear what she was saying. Stopping in the middle of the conversation I asked her, "Aren't you going to tell your boy to stop drumming the harp strings?"

"Oh no," she smiled, "he will soon get tired of it and stop by himself."

By that time the boy was practically jumping on the pedals of the harp. I turned, and strictly and firmly commanded him to stop, to get out of the house and play outside. He looked unbelievingly at me, and meekly walked out.

I told the mother, "You can bring up your child in freedom in your own house, but you cannot let him destroy a musical instrument in our house." She was so mortally offended that I scarcely ever saw her again.

We have gone through hundreds of these typical experiences of the "new school" created by "new" psychologists who claim that children must be allowed to express themselves. It is no wonder that the teen-ager therefore, by a "natural" course of events becomes the ruling power of our society.

But as usual in all the strata of our life, we find sensitive and perceptive teen-agers with faith and aspiration and love of the search for things more excellent. It is such youth that will cause a necessary revolution. They are the leaven that will save the future life of America.

Chapter 16

The "Intelligence Quotient" and aptitude tests still persist as the measure of development and inclinations, particularly of the young person. To judge people by their momentary reactions is an uncertain measurement. So much depends upon the state of mind and feeling, the physical conditions, the surrounding circumstances; I. Q. and aptitude tests can hardly lead toward correct judgment. It is impossible to judge anyone in a temporary state and since most of us live in temporary, constantly changing, states, we have to know people for a long time before we can define their abilities. Through contact with them and the things they do, we may eventually arrive at a certain evaluation of them.

The change that takes place from day to day is so pronounced that a sudden crystallizing incident such as a test may have no bearing on true ability. Judgment by isolated incidents, completely cut away from the fabric of life, can produce no clear picture of anyone's capabilities or character. Even some accidental circumstances of the day before might cause, for instance, dullness, nervousness, fatigue—none of them characteristic. The complexity of people is far too great; a test is apt to show some entirely non-characteristic picture as if it were the whole human being.

Almost a thousand young people have come and gone through the gates of Taliesin. After three months or so, the apprentice shows some features which define him —his weaknesses as well as his strength. But it has sometimes taken a full year before we were really sure of both his talent and his character.

In our experience over the years of conducting the Taliesin Fellowship, Mr. Wright and I tried early to appraise the apprentices that came to join our work. They had gone to various schools; they were of various ages. Mr. Wright and I frequently received well written letters applying for attendance. Both of us would look forward to the interviews.

Often the interviews were quite satisfactory and the drawings presented would be good. Then in the course of the first months of their stay there would occasionally emerge unsuspected negative features of character—an absence of good feeling, of understanding, of cooperation; sometimes downright lack of intelligence and, what was more astonishing, a lack of architectural talent as well—none of which was evident at the time of the interviews.

On the other hand letters would be written with little correlation, and even in the interviews the young men or women would make a poor impression in almost every way. But after a while at Taliesin they would blossom in spirit and intelligence, frequently revealing considerable architectural gifts. When given impetus by encouragement in an atmosphere of growth, they would truly thrive.

How often now I find myself confronted with an unknown entity, faced with the responsibility of making a correct judgment. Among one of my interviews, I remember a young man who had come a great distance. He had difficulty in expressing himself and was nervous beyond any reason. I was uncertain in accepting him and almost said "no." Then I asked him if he had already brought his belongings; when he said that he had, my nerve left me—he stayed.

After a few months, finding himself among friends, he relaxed and was liked by everyone. He proved to be a gifted and a responsible worker; enthusiastic by temperament and naturally honest; and he even lost his nervous mannerisms. To think that I might have closed the door to him—

This experience confirmed more strongly than ever how hard it is to pass judgment on anyone. There are no adequate tests, no measurements; recommendation is unreliable because it is often out of kindness that people are recommended.

The only sound measurement left to us is watchfulness, patience, and kindness. And while giving an apprentice the right direction along the line of his talent and character we simply hope for the best.

Chapter 17

Among the many social problems arising with great rapidity in most of the so-called civilized countries, and one of the most serious that is facing us now, is divorce.

The divorce rate is rising rapidly, particularly in America, and its effect touches all of us. We hear from pastors in the churches that many people come to them with their problems, really with one basic intent in mind—divorce. Instead of trying to make adjustments, they are driven instantly to think of divorce as the only way out of the family conflict and their incapability of getting along with one another.

Social forces as they are now composed stand against marriage. By making divorce an easy thing we have endangered the institution of marriage. In some states it takes only three weeks to obtain one; in some states immediate re-marriage is permissible. Such ease in obtaining divorce has imperilled the possibility of bridging difficulties, of overcoming friction and antagonism between married couples. Within their psyche they know, consciously or unconsciously, that they can always get a divorce. I have heard young people say,

"Well, I think I'll marry her," or "I think I'll marry him. After all, if it doesn't work out I can get a divorce"— a psychological condition that is bound to defeat marriage before the people go into the union.

I have tried to impress upon many a young couple who intended to marry that they should not marry with the idea "if it doesn't work I can always get my freedom back." How could such an attitude possibly bring hope or faith into the future? This has been an increasingly weak link in the marriage status for some years now. I would not be surprised if Aldous Huxley's prediction came true: life without the responsibility of a man and his wife to each other, without recognition of duty on the part of parents toward their children—nothing to bind anyone. Should any suffering in this new world appear, it could easily be eradicated by drugs which would set the mind at peace, even elevate it into a state of exultation; thus violating all the laws of decency in human conduct.

I would not be surprised if, after this dreadful phase is over, we will once more go back to marriage as a sacred institution indissoluble by divorce, to the state of our ancestors when a divorced person was a social outcast.

The world seems to move in cycles. Because the social structure changes continually, a variety of trials are always ahead of us. But if the social forms of one decade do not fit those of another, the basic principle should remain constant. When two people decide to marry they should consider their marriage as permanent. It is fortunate that we still admire a long lasting marriage. Love grows with years of struggle, effort and even friction. In love the very struggles, efforts and frictions culminate in victory—the marks of human dignity and of human faith.

The false marriage of necessity is to be feared because a man forced to marry is bound to abuse his wife for the rest of their married life for having married her merely to save her social face. Though that kind of marriage has seldom worked out, there are a great many of them still. And too many marriages are accidental—without thought or plan for the future. I sometimes wonder if the Orientals were not right when they chose the bride or bridegroom for their children. We once had with us an Egyptian couple, Salah and Samiha Zeitoon, with their lovely little daughter, Samia. One time Samiha told me how she married her husband. "My father and mother and Salah's father and mother decided when we were children that we should marry, and, oh Mrs. Wright, I was so frightened and worried the day I was to meet Salah. But when I saw him I just knew right away that he was the man for me and I would have no other." Their marriage was successful —they strove together for a better life. When Salah decided to study achitecture at Taliesin they left Egypt and came with their little daughter to us. Theirs were happy years.

One day at tea I teased Samiha, "I understand that in Egypt a man can have several wives. How would you feel if your Salah had another wife?"

She looked at me with her dark eyes and, flashing her lovely smile, said, "Mrs. Wright, if he had another wife, I would kill him!"

Her life with Salah is a happy life today. When Mr.

Wright and I went to Egypt we visited Salah and Samiha. They had another boy, and little Samia, now fifteen years old, was a beautiful girl. In general the married couples we met in Cairo seemed to have more stability. Perhaps we are not yet ready as developed individuals to have the wisdom of correct choice in marriage. But I am not one to say that predestined marriages may be the solution of our social system. With the laws making divorce so accessible to us today, however, it may not hurt us to stop a while and think on this constant threat to the institution of marriage.

Chapter 18

The secret of satisfaction which all of us seek lies in the correct inner attitude toward all life, and not in our outward surroundings. Whatever we are within us, whatever view we take of any situation that arises, it is in that view that happiness or unhappiness is contained—not in any actual occurrence. It seems difficult for us to comprehend that attitude is everything, that it is by our attitude toward life and our position on earth that we either succeed or lose. It is by our attitude that we either end our life in loneliness, facing old age with horror, or we change whatever happens to us into an act of some goodness.

We are bound together. And as we generate in one another a positive attitude toward everything that happens we intensify within us the spark, the interest in everything that takes place.

But it is very easy to turn life into a curse, to regard it only as a series of terrifying difficulties piling up to defeat our purpose. People accomplish something within themselves who see living as a superior act, even a divine act—life a gift bestowed on those who walk on earth. One should treat such a gift with something more than constant distrust and existence on alternating planes of horror and despair.

It is within our own power to do so. Nothing impedes our inner progress more than our inability to correct our attitude from within and our waiting for some outward condition to change it for us. The misfortune that ensues from human relations lies in this inability to correct one's attitude. In attitudes, which we ourselves can form, lies the secret of good life. Our attitude determines whether we live in misery or live with a peaceful acceptance that our life is a series of changes in light and shadow from birth to death. The consequences of these inevitable changes will depend solely on our attitude toward them. Many squirm through life's difficulties, others find satisfaction in the challenge.

Our attitudes prepare the way for the future. The present generation, living in inner disorder, cannot hope that its descendants will profit by its misery and firm disbelief in everything! How can future generations profit when the present one lives in anguish and in futile pursuits of oblivion? How can we give to the future faith and hope when we know only the misery of a life heavily loaded with distrusting attitudes? Future generations could not possibly benefit spiritually from the results of our advance in this material, industrial, mechanical and scientific world. That is not what they will need. They will need the inheritance of a life within—to be contained and intensified during the procession of their years. This is the great inheritance that can be passed on to the next generation, instead of more and more mechanical devices to insure the physical comfort of those to come. We are in danger of grinding our inner vitality by feeding it into the wheels of the machine, and thus tampering with our soul. In the insatiable desire for more material development, the interior substance of the soul vanishes. We must take all the warnings from whichever direction they come to us if we are not to be devoured and ground under the pressure of our material age.

We must not lose the most important aim that a human being lives for—peace within—that peace which is generated by love and faith.

Chapter 19

Among the worst sins of which we are all guilty is that of taking for granted our relationships with our families, our friends, our country. We take for granted even life itself. Engrossed by trivialities and set patterns we miss our vital relationships and the vital expressions of ourselves during our day. Much as we may try to be selective in the choice of our friends, our literature or our entertainment, most frequently we simply yield to the pattern of the day. Burdened as we are by the technicalities of our present civilization, we take little time to give nourishment to the essential needs of our spirit.

Since I have been reading from the manuscripts of Mr. Wright's lectures to the Taliesin Fellowship, many have said to me that for some reason now when I read to them they understand better than they did when Mr. Wright himself spoke.

"Your attention is intensified because he is no longer with us," I answer. "You value every word of his more highly—therefore you understand more clearly.

"You take people for granted. You took even Mr. Wright for granted because you knew that every Sunday you would hear him speak. But now, when he is

not here, you cling to every word that I read. Therefore his ideas and his observations contain deeper mean-
ings for you.

"And it would be good to take notice of this now so
that while you are living all together you may put more
of that quality of sharpened perception and power of
appreciation in your daily contact with one another.
Do not lose out by taking everyone for granted. Do not
fall into the pattern of those who only years later wrote
how much they had missed at Taliesin and what fruit-
ful years theirs could have been had they but realized
their great opportunity."

How frequently we regret not having seen more of the
friends we care for. They move to another town, to
another part of the country, and a feeling of sadness
overcomes us. We wish we had disentangled ourselves
from our chores and had found time to give to our
friends.

Technical activity submerges interior impulses. We
ourselves become pretty much patternized and the
rigidity of the form of our day often set us in the direction of retrogression. We let go of the life essential to
our spirit. Our salvation lies in awareness of these
dangers.

We are keenly aware of dangers we encounter on the
highway. We sit at the wheel of the automobile watching carefully for the signs, "stop," "slow," "crossroad,"
"curve"—yet how little of this degree of awareness we
exercise toward the safety of our spirit.

We indulge in poverty-stricken attitudes toward
others, always expecting something for nothing, not
realizing that we receive only that which we give. In

the language of physical science: action and reaction are always equal. Yet it seems difficult for us to believe that this law is the same in the realm of the spirit.

If we indulge in a form of entertainment which leaves us depressed, exhausted, drained—it would serve us well to register that state and stop before falling into the same pattern the next time. It is never too late to repair one's errors. By repairing them, our vision becomes clearer as to what step is to be taken next. All of us make errors; but we know that we can change. When looking back it is good to remember just where the line of principle was interrupted, and where we have to pick it up again and continue with faith so as not to damage our spirit.

We can all strive to achieve this simple precept: live in such a way that we hurt no one including ourselves.

Chapter 20

"For whosoever hath, to him shall be given, and he shall have more abundance: but whosoever hath not, from him shall be taken away even that he hath." This statement of Christ has baffled many people. Mr. Wright interpreted these words thus: . . . "Rather than the quality of the individual, you are being offered the quantitative character of the mob, if you want to reduce it to its absurd limit. And there is the whole world struggle—in that simple statement of fact. That explains the rise of Communism—the religion of the 'have-not' as against the religion of the 'have'—if you translate the 'have' to the things of the soul and the spirit instead of the things of the body."

The "haves" are those who have something to give from within. They are spiritually developed. And the "have-nots" are the sterile ones whose metallic minds, mechanically clicking, produce little real thought. The inventiveness of the mind is merely one consequence catching itself to another consequence to produce another consequence with no creative aim or even a creative tendency. Invention and science are predominant in our world today. Soon we will begin to be more and more aware of how dangerous a time we are living in—the time of the "have-nots." We may know by our mind only, but gradually we will know with all our being, how fearful our situation is without the spirit to connect us with the progressive, inventive uses of the mind. Mind without the control of the spirit will destroy life.

The "have-nots" succeed because they are not motivated by any high ethical ideal as the "haves" are. They seek the easy way and it is easier for them to succeed in what they are pursuing on their lower level.

"In relation to architecture," Mr. Wright said, "anybody can stand up four sticks together and put a box on top of it, then bore holes through the box, and there is the building in the new, so-called 'International style.'" Those are the "have-nots." They have no imagination. They have no creative spirit. They can quickly sprinkle the earth with those buildings because they require no creative effort. Creative spirit struggles to produce a beautiful form, wanting to perfect the next one and the next—ever changing of forms. Through the desire to create new and better conditions in order to simplify and beautify our life on earth, the spirit is ever refreshed, acquiring more imperishable substance.

There naturally exists little possibility of growth in those who apply no effort in their lives. And yet they can populate the earth, and they can make the life of those with noble spirit very uncomfortable. They can impede the influence of great ideas, but they cannot destroy them. This declaration of Christ has been a great enigma to people. Why should He say, "For whosoever hath, to him shall be given, and he shall have more abundance: but whosoever hath not, from him shall be taken away even that he hath"? The latter will be destroyed.

It is hard to visualize humanity rolling on the power of hydrogen and atom bombs very long without some catastrophe overtaking everything living, unless men of spirit fight the loose metallic patterns of the mind. Spirit has a tremendous power of benevolent radiation.

Good and constructive thoughts create more good and constructive thoughts, not only through the written and spoken word, building, sculpture, painting or music, but also through their radiations. Thoughts have the capacity of perpetuating themselves, maintaining and raising humanity to a higher level. But expressions of great ideas in concrete form are needed to complete our development on earth.

The presence of Mr. Wright's spirit is manifest in his vibrant thoughts. These thoughts have their wavelengths—they generate power in others. The waves of these thoughts will never cease to exist; they are imperishable. And of course the higher the mind rises, the more powerful are the thoughts. The power of Mr. Wright's thoughts will carry on into the infinite future.

Some great future historian will feel his thoughts. The greatest historian is the one who can feel history, not the one who merely records the dates of events. That is why we have so few true historians. They, too, have to be highly developed individuals. In all forms, all professions, what we need today is the development of individuality. They are the true "haves" of Christ's teachings.

One has to struggle to acquire individuality. Individuality seems to have its roots in hardships and in difficulties. The remnants of an animal nature in us make us seek the easy way in everything we do. Yet in our hearts, deep in our thoughts, we know that only through hardships do we really live as strong individuals. We add strength instead of detracting from it. We become the "haves" of Christ's teaching.

EPILOGUE

It is by Providence that Frank Lloyd Wright was placed in just the right kind of environment to correspond to his hereditary and God-given qualities. His strong bloodline on his mother's side, combined with the highly intellectual, scholarly trend on his father's side, produced a perfectly balanced entity.

His childhood years spent both in the city and on the farm were just right for his growth. His fiery imagination as a child might have done him harm had he stayed in the limiting activity of city life. His imaginative nature was balanced with life and hard work on the Wisconsin farm. To this was added the poetry of oaks, pines and birches; picturesque brooks bending their way through the gentle, friendly soft hills; meadows covered with dogtooth violets, beebalm, Queen Anne's lace, vervain, fireweed, wild red lilies; fields of wheat and oats where he worked strengthening his physical and spiritual muscle. He grew in the freedom of Nature listening to its secret words.

Later in his life these secrets never left him. They were consumed by his system to create the buildings which were as natural as the wildflowers, the rivers and the brooks, his beloved fields and meadows, always belonging where they were placed—even on crowded avenues of large cities. He called his architecture "organic" because it is alive with spirit. "Part is to part as part is to the whole," he said. "Only as all is one does anything live. When form and function become one— the spirit of life enters."

He stands as a giant among the generations of men because not only was his physical body harmonious but his mind was obedient to his will, his intellect brilliant and his spirit built of a fierce fiery fibre which nothing could defeat. Death cannot destroy him. His projection left on earth will speak for thousands of years to those who understand.

He stopped before nothing in his structural concepts. If it was a cliff, he swiftly adapted it to his building. If it was an ocean, he used it to serve him, and the waves respected his wishes and struck the rocks beneath his house with just the right force. If a magnificent tree happened to stand in his way as he designed, he put a gentle arm around the tree, keeping it to adorn the dwelling. If he liked the top of a green hill, he swept his building around it in order to preserve the flowing perfect lines created by nature. If he hung a cantilever, he projected it as far as he pleased, and it always stood for him.

An architect said, "This could stand for no one else but for Frank Lloyd Wright." Such miracles were natural to him. The greater the problem, the obstacles, the greater was his power of overcoming them. He could weave himself like a cobra around a mountain range and he could rear like a flying Pegasus ready to take off to the highest pinnacle. His buildings are that way. He could be poised like a swan on a lake, and his building would float in the atmosphere.

He was like the Grand Canyon; complex, rugged, colorful, dug deep into the soil while the jagged ridges reach the sky. Such are his buildings.

He saw the minute detail and the whole at once; he built and completed the structure in his mind. There was no division in him and that is the way his buildings are.

He was essentially a conqueror. He lived to fight and he was certain of his victory. In the midst of the most complex situations where everyone and everything seemed to stand against his plan, he unfolded gigantic wings, and the power of his wings was so great that he swept into flight everyone close to him. And so strong was his faith in the truth of his action that even his enemies, while cursing, bent down under his irresistible power.

He was the very core of optimism. He made miracles happen through the faith he possessed while others gave up and lost—in doubt.

Another architect at a dinner asked him, "How did you get to build a modern house for clients who were bred, hatched and raised in a colonial atmosphere? What did you do, hypnotize them?"

Mr. Wright looked composed and said evenly, "No. I simply told them the truth. There is nothing so hypnotic as the truth."

Nothing stood in his way. "Tireless study of nature is the secret of all success," he said. "I have the secret of nature. I find the solution of a problem within the problem itself. While others look for aid outside—I find it within."

I have met no man to surpass him in his amazingly practical and superb common sense. In his way of planning, building and living, he possessed the secret key that other men failed even to look for. I have seen the most pragmatic, practical men of the world come up against his exposition, to find themselves lost, mowed down by his practical power. It was hard for them to admit defeat. They shook their heads, "It will not work." But it always worked. Even then they still shook their heads, "This works only for Frank Lloyd Wright," they said.

His power of practical perception was so natural, so complete, that they could not encompass one-millionth part of it.

I have also seen engineers shaking their heads and wondering if the building would stand up. Some of them still believed that the roof should have more reinforcement or the cantilever more support. But their suggestions were almost always caught and thrown out by Mr. Wright, outraged at their lack of faith in him. The engineers were uneasy in his presence because they feared to lose their stand—and they inevitably lost it. He reached beyond their mathematical conclusions. So he changed the laws and rules of construction, forever creating new engineering formulas which are taught in the colleges as standard laws of building today.

He was the most practical visionary who has ever lived. With his sublimely developed instinct, common sense, intuition, reasoning power, combined with unlimited flight of imagination, he represented the finest specimen yet born among the generations of men.

At times when he turned white with fury, his eyes were molten steel. His whole face and body became saturated with a force beyond human. He was terrifying to behold, and in a way breathtaking as a vision from another world. I then moved along with him, speeding up my own rate just enough to slow him down, unbeknown to him. And then when he sat at his drafting board, he would draw with power and speed and the concentration of a supernatural being. And when he had finished, he was gay, companionable, witty, relaxed and even-lined like the undisturbed quiet surface of a great ocean.

When I struck the thinnest spark to his imagination it was set aflame within that very moment.

One day in our desert camp in Arizona, when we were standing together on an enclosed corridor-terrace connecting our quarters with the large living room, I said to him, "Don't you think it would be more beautiful if we did not have this wall separating us from the patio-garden—instead you could build long steps leading down into it? We would feel the patio closer to us then."

Instantly he called out, "Ted, bring the crowbar and a couple of boys."

"Wait." I said, "it is just lunch time!"

"It won't hurt us to eat later," he said, and down came the wall—the wreckage and the dust flying into our own living quarters. He then changed another wall, and the room, and the fireplace and the ceiling and the openings.

He was a most flexible, most plastic man. Unaware of time, he lived through sorrows or tragedies, joys or humiliations, remaining ever young, fresh—always poised for the next action. Believing with Heraclitus that there is only one unchangeable law, the Law of Change, he embodied this law. He was forever changing, remaining unchangeable. Opposites met within him in perfect proportion. They were reconciled and consumed by him as one. The Law of Cruelty that exists in Nature he blended smoothly with the Law of Love.

He believed in God, but he did not wish to relinquish the Nature on which he put a capital "N." Love he attributed to God, though resisting the personalized God; he in a way reconciled this within himself as an Idea. He contributed divine attributes to this Idea, continuing it as Understanding, as Love—thus connecting it with the image of Man. These two images, God and Man, merged in him. He loathed to give up one for another. His concept of religion was many-dimensional—extremely complex—but the idea of God, whatever vision it represented to him personally, was deeply rooted in him.

His love of man was undeniable, as was his love of God. But when he spoke of man and God, he had them so intertwined, especially when he added his love of Nature, that it is difficult for anyone to express his innermost faith and vision. How difficult it must have been for him whose inner world represented a whole cosmos to express himself in terms of life.